Praise for

The Place We Make

"*The Place We Make* is coming into the world at a very unique time in history. As the news fills with book banning and the dissolution of DEI programs, this book refreshingly points to another way. Sarah has done a beautiful job weaving painful historical moments with her faith in a way that invites you in and causes you to think. I particularly love the consideration and care that this book provides by quoting so many thinkers of color in a quest for truth and honesty."

—ROBERT MONSON, enfleshed co-director, writer, and theologian

"With grace and transparency, Sarah Sanderson extends to readers an invitation into sorrow and empathy to feel another person's story and to further reimagine our own stories too. *The Place We Make* is not only an important read for White folks, Pacific Northwesterners, Christians, and the spiritually curious, but for anyone who needs to flip history's hidden records upside down."

—CARA MEREDITH, author of *The Color of Life*

"We don't know what we don't know until what we don't know shocks us into reality. In her exquisite debut, *The Place We Make*, Sarah L. Sanderson comes face-to-face with her ancestral roots in a specific place: Oregon City, Oregon. It is where her forebearers made their home—but at a steep price. Sanderson writes, 'This town was not just meant to be quintessentially Christian and American. It was also designed, legislated, and enforced to be a White utopia.' The current

American zeitgeist would have us believe that we are self-made individuals free of past influences, good or bad. But through her own story, written in beautiful prose, Sarah demonstrates that we do not live in a historical vacuum. On the contrary, the specters of American history will only be laid to rest when we acknowledge their presence in the past and present. A White utopia isn't a utopia for anyone else. This is a must-read."

—MARLENA GRAVES, author of *The Way Up Is Down*

"History is never just history, as Sarah Sanderson shows in this gripping narrative of the way her own story—along with her own place—is connected to that of someone from long ago whose life, experiences, and status couldn't be more different from her own. And yet, in telling this story, Sanderson eloquently and movingly shows how our stories are interconnected across time, even the stories (or the sides of the stories) we are rarely told. This is a beautiful, painful, and moving account of the past, which Sanderson tells through an honest examination of her own present. *The Place We Make* offers a compelling model for the way in which we all might understand our own stories and the way these stories are shaped—for good and for ill—by those who came before us."

—KAREN SWALLOW PRIOR, PHD, author of
The Evangelical Imagination

"Sanderson's questions in *The Place We Make* caused me to think carefully and left me with a lengthy set of my own. Few will dare to make an exploration so honest and humble as the one in these pages."

—MELISSA MOORE, co-author of *Now That Faith Has Come*

THE
PLACE
WE
MAKE

THE PLACE WE MAKE

Breaking the Legacy of Legalized Hate

Sarah L. Sanderson

Foreword by Chanté Griffin

WATERBROOK

Published in the United States by WaterBrook, an imprint of Random House,
a division of Penguin Random House LLC.

WATERBROOK and colophon are registered trademarks of
Penguin Random House LLC.

Library of Congress Cataloging-in-Publication Data
Names: Sanderson, Sarah L., author.
Title: The place we make: breaking the legacy of legalized hate / Sarah L. Sanderson.
Description: Colorado Springs: WaterBrook, [2023] |
Includes bibliographical references and index.
Identifiers: LCCN 2023006259 | ISBN 9780593444733 (hardcover) |
ISBN 9780593444740 (ebook)
Subjects: LCSH: Race relations. | Equality.
Classification: LCC HT1521 .S2735 2023 | DDC 305.8—dc23/eng/20230330
LC record available at https://lccn.loc.gov/2023006259

Printed in the United States of America on acid-free paper

waterbrookmultnomah.com

2 4 6 8 9 7 5 3 1

FIRST EDITION

Book design by Ralph Fowler

Most WaterBrook books are available at special quantity discounts for bulk purchase for
premiums, fundraising, and corporate and educational needs by organizations, churches,
and businesses. Special books or book excerpts also can be created to fit specific needs. For
details, contact specialmarketscms@penguinrandomhouse.com.

The author is donating 90 percent of the proceeds from this book to:

Oregon Black Pioneers

Equal Justice Initiative

The Crete Collective

The Red Door Project

Native American Youth and
Family Center of Portland

and other organizations that
benefit people of color.

for Loy
who is finally done running

and for Jayedin
who's just getting started

No free Negro, or Mulatto, not residing in this state
at the time of the adoption of this constitution,
shall come, reside, or be within this state,
or hold any real estate, or make any contracts, or
    maintain any suit therein;
and the Legislative Assembly shall provide by penal
    laws,
for the removal, by public officers, of all such Negroes,
    and Mulattos,
and for their effectual exclusion from the state,
and for the punishment of persons who shall bring
    them into the state,
or employ, or harbor them.

—amendment to the Oregon State Constitution, 1857,
    Oregon State Archives

The only thing about Oregon that is unique
is that they were bold enough to write it down.

—Walidah Imarisha, "Why Aren't There More Black
    People in Oregon? A Hidden History"

Foreword

As the United States struggles to find its footing during this era of racial reckoning, throughout the book publishing industry and beyond, a question looms large: Is there space for White voices? Given that the publishing industry has historically marginalized voices of color, should there be space for a White woman to write a book that documents racism toward Black people and Native Americans, especially when said racism was proliferated by her relatives?

These questions are critical. Yet I humbly suggest there are two more questions to ask: Should there be space for voices that cry out to repent and repair? And, *Who* ultimately benefits when these voices speak out? I believe that answering the latter questions helps answer the former ones.

I met Sarah L. Sanderson in the summer of 2022 when she attended the Writing With God virtual retreat I co-lead with poet Velynn Brown, a fellow Black writer. Velynn had invited Sarah, who was knee-deep in writing *The Place We Make,* to set up a consultation with me during the retreat. I imagine Sarah wanted to meet with me because I'm a journalist who writes extensively about how race intersects with various aspects of U.S. culture, including faith.

During our time together, Sarah's internal turmoil was evident: A part of her felt drawn to writing this book, but another part wondered if hers was the right voice to tell this story: *Am I doing what my ancestors have done before me? Taking ownership and command of stories and lands that aren't ours to touch in the first place?*

In *The Place We Make,* Sarah examines Oregon's exclusion laws that banned Black people from living within its borders and details how, in 1851, a successful businessman named Jacob Vanderpool was expelled from living and making a living in Oregon City—a town only minutes from Sarah's current home—*simply* because he was Black. Throughout the book, Sarah takes readers back in time to witness how the intersecting forces of racism, greed, and silence forcibly removed Vanderpool from Oregon City, prevented other Black people from settling in the state, and stole land from the Clackamas Tribe who resided there.

While speaking with Sarah and reading *The Place We Make,* I was struck by her humility toward the book's topics. Instead of positioning herself as a heroine, she took the posture of a learner and truth-teller, regardless of how bad it makes her or her family look. As a reader and fellow writer, I appreciated her candor and vulnerability. And as a Christian, I especially appreciated how she publicly grappled with how to repair what she and her ancestors have breached.

Should there be space for voices that cry out to repent and repair? Absolutely. After reading *The Place We Make,* I believe Sarah L. Sanderson is one of those voices.

And to answer the question about *who* ultimately benefits when these voices speak out, well, we *all* benefit: displaced Black Oregonians, all of Oregon's residents, racial justice advocates, as well as students of history who want to connect the dots between our past and our present. (I, for one, can count on my hand the number of Black people I saw in the Beaver State the one time I visited. Now I know why.) History buffs, activists, and those who seek to repair the breaches racism forged will also appreciate this tenderly delivered book. It's a beautiful rendering of an ugly history, a worthy read among the myriad of race books published in recent years. I am honored to introduce you to it.

—Chanté Griffin, advocate,
journalist, and author

Contents

Author's Note

Many writers working on the subject of racism in America capitalize *Black* but not *white*, citing various reasons for doing so. These range from the claim that *white* does not denote a "shared culture and history," to the argument that leaving it uncapitalized reflects a desire to withhold from white people the "respect, pride, and celebration" that is extended to the Black community with a capital *B*. For many years, I wrote with a capital *B* for *Black* and a lowercase *w* for *white*.

But I have chosen in this book to emulate scholars such as Kwame Anthony Appiah, Eve Ewing, Nell Irvin Painter, Imani Perry, and Chanequa Walker-Barnes, who insist on the capitalization of both *Black* and *White*. Leaving the *w* uncapitalized, Ewing wrote, is "reinforcing the dangerous myth that White people in America do not have a racial identity." After four hundred years of racialization, being White means something. My grappling with *what* it means, exactly, is the very subject of this book.

Another stylistic choice I'd like to point out is the omission of reference numbers that would direct you to citations. Though the citations are still in the endnotes, they are tied to page numbers and keywords rather than superscript numbers in the text. In this way, I hope to facilitate uninterrupted engagement with the story for all readers, while still providing access to citations for those who want to find my sources.

Introduction

Let us take a knife
And cut the world in two—
And see what worms are eating
At the rind.

   —Langston Hughes, "Tired,"
   The Collected Poems of Langston Hughes

What do you see when you lift your eyes from this book?

Someone's shoulder, perhaps, as they brush past you in the bookstore? Library shelves? Tired bodies folded into subway seats? Your grandmother's quilt draped over your toes? The edge of your beach towel or the ever-shifting edge where sand meets water?

Wherever you are in the world—whether surrounded by evergreens or palm trees or a thicket of office towers, whether sitting in a waiting room or an aisle seat or nestled on your living room couch—thank you for bringing me along to this place you call *here*. I do not know it the way you do. I do not know the name of the baby whose cry will light up the monitor any second now, or the names of the cows in your barn, or the name of the woman who drives your bus. I don't know the names of the laborers who built the building in which you are sitting, or the names of the children who played in that very spot thousands of years before anyone thought to build there at all. I can tell you only what I discovered when I began to be curious about *my* place. This is the story of what I learned when I began to wonder about the place where I live: who made it, and why, and how it all came to be.

When you leave the thought-place we make together in the sharing of these pages and return to the real place of dishes and deadlines and bills, I hope you will carry some of my questions with you.

I wonder what you will find if you do.

Originally, I wanted to write about Jacob Vanderpool—the only Black man living in the tiny frontier town of Oregon City in 1851. Oregon was the only state admitted to the Union with anti-Black exclusion laws on its books; Jacob Vanderpool was the only person ever expelled from Oregon under the application of those laws. He was, in fact, the only person in the history of the United States ever convicted and punished solely for the crime of being Black.

The singularity of that fact riveted me: the *only* state, the *only* man. Throughout the vast history of injustice rolling down like a mighty river across this nation, from century to century and sea to shining sea, here, I thought, was a story small enough for me to hold.

But as I began to ask questions, I grew concerned that the evidence available for Jacob Vanderpool's story might be *too* small to give a satisfactory account. The social ramifications of his story were certainly immense. His life itself had surely been as large and full and valuable as every other human life. But history seemed to have hidden its records.

The known facts were maddeningly few. Vanderpool had been a sailor. He turned his hand to hotel management in June 1851. He stood trial in August under the Exclusion Law. By the end of September, he'd been expelled from the Oregon Territory. I dug and poked but could not discover where Vanderpool had lived before he came to Oregon or where he went after; nothing was said about whom he had loved or what he had cherished. It seemed that the life of the only person legally exiled from Oregon had not won the attention of the keepers of the state's annals. Though not unusual for the time, the omission itself felt to me like another indignity—a second wrong.

In contrast to how little we know about Jacob Vanderpool, however, there was a great deal in the historical record about the men who had successfully conspired against him. There was John McLoughlin, the Founder; Theophilus Magruder, the Treasure Hunter; Thomas Nelson, the Judge; and Ezra Fisher, the Pastor— all men whose lives history has not forgotten. Oregon celebrates her wagon-train heroes with statues and plaques, museum exhibitions and elementary school field trips. Ezra Fisher's name is painted on the wall in the Senate chambers at the Oregon State Capitol; John McLoughlin's and Thomas Nelson's names are displayed in the House. Yet these famously lauded pioneers had moved—in some cases, specifically and deliberately; in others, with silent complicity—to oust a Black man from their midst.

Why?

I began to wonder if this was the story for me to tell—not *what* happened to Jacob Vanderpool but *why* it happened. I could not speak for a man who was the object of racism. But perhaps I could look squarely at those who directed their racism at him, twisting and bending the levers of society to expel a neighbor whose only crime was the darkness of his skin. Who were these people who had acted in this egregious way? And why had they done it? "The scholarship that looks into the mind, imagination, and behavior of slaves is valuable," wrote Toni Morrison. "But equally valuable is a serious intellectual effort to see what racial ideology does to the mind, imagination, and behavior of masters." How had racism warped the minds, imaginations, and behaviors of those who took it upon themselves to master Oregon?

As I tried to learn what had shaped the people who had so deeply influenced the place I call home, I realized my journey would not only take me to nineteenth-century Oregon. I would also have to travel further back, to the very origins of the racialized story that human beings have been telling about ourselves, and further out, to see how racism had shaped my nation and the world.

And, I discovered, I would need to go further in—to explore the secret depths of my own heart. For, like the early settlers of Oregon City, I am White. My mind, imagination, and behavior have also been shaped by the racial ideology of the society in which I live: the society that those White men of long ago had a hand in making. As I examined their racist deeds, my study forced me to look again and again at my own face in the mirror.

I am a daughter of Oregon. I was born here. After decades away, I have recently returned. Some branches of my family tree trace their arrival in the Northwest all the way back to those first wagon trains. When I began this investigation, I knew I was related by blood and marriage to one of the White men whose stories I wanted to tell. In the course of my study, I learned that I share a common ancestor with a second man as well.

This is my place. These are my people. I may not be able to answer for what they did. But by the grace of God, I can at least begin to ask.

By the grace of God is not merely a rhetorical flourish. Throughout this book, my work springs from my conviction as a Christian. I want to be clear about this from the outset for three reasons. First, I want you to know what kind of book you are getting yourself into. Though I write as a Christian, I do not intend to write *only* for Christians, and I hope that if you are not the kind of person who regularly picks up Christian books, your curiosity might impel you to keep reading anyway. I will speak as clearly as possible so that whether or not you are familiar with the practice of faith, you might understand what I am trying to say.

Second, I want to be clear about my faith because I believe it is past time for White American Christians to practice thinking and talking about matters of race. Works like Willie James Jennings's *The Christian Imagination: Theology and the Origins of Race* and Jemar Tisby's *The Color of Compromise: The Truth About the American Church's Complicity in Racism* explain how the church has historically not only condoned but often engineered the evils of White supremacy. We must reckon with this legacy.

I am certainly not claiming to be the first person to lead this charge. Many White Christian leaders have far more knowledge on the subject than I do. But my experience with people in the pews (of whom I am one) is that many of us are so afraid to say the wrong thing that we can hardly bring ourselves to say anything at all. What I hope to bring you in this book is not the advice of yet another expert but simply the story of how I myself was confused, scared, and in need of forgiveness, and how I inched my way forward.

And that brings me to the third reason I need to tell you that I am a Christian: because I don't know if I could have overcome the fear and shame I felt in approaching this subject if I didn't *believe*, down to my toes, that there is a God whose heart for us overflows with grace. I do not know how else I could have summoned the courage to undertake this work—to examine injustices perpetrated by my own ancestors; to trace the lines running straight from the racist histories of so many White people in America to the realities I found lurking in my own heart; to tiptoe into the chilly currents of my own hidden racism—without the belief that the God who loves justice also loves *me*.

Some think forgiveness is a panacea—that those who drop their sins at the foot of the cross are merely imagining for themselves a world in which they never need face the consequences of their own actions. I believe the opposite is true. I never could have begun to face the enormity of my own or my people's sins if I didn't believe in grace. After all, as the apostle Paul wrote nearly two thousand years ago, it is the kindness of God that leads us to repentance.

No, forgiveness does not always mean forgetting. Forgiveness means, instead, that we are pursued by a love that is larger than space and older than time—a love that surrounds us and whispers that we are safe enough to begin to remember.

Prologue

First came the lava.

It hurtled up from the planet's core: red-hot liquid bursting forth with power and force, rolling and sliding over hundreds of miles of fresh-cracked earth until it cooled and slowed and stopped and became rock. Faraway volcanoes popped and rumbled; furious magma rushed and slid. Millennium after millennium, lava flowed and lava flowed. For two million years, the lava flowed. And, layer by layer, there was land.

Next came the floods.

An ice dam broke on a distant lake; an ocean of water raced across the plateau. The deluge pushed between mountains, pooled in valleys, carved gorges, and snaked along riverbeds until the very shapes of the hills were nothing but the memory of water. For three thousand years, ice froze and broke, froze and broke, froze and broke again, spilling cataclysms of glacial torrents every time. The water buffeted the rocks, rubbed at the basalt, and wore away the stone until the floods had formed a path for the water to follow on its journey from the snowmelt to the sea. And there was river.

When the floodwaters receded, the river remained: a sinuous ribbon pulsing through flatland. The river rolled gently through the valley until it came *here,* this one last great hurdle of volcanic rock. Now it flings itself over, a million flashing droplets at a time. More water flows over this falls than almost any other on the continent. All through the valley, the water gurgles. But here, at the bow-shaped waterfall—this joyous clash of land and river—the water roars.

This is what God did.

It was God—or as the Clowwewalla say, the ancient hero Coyote—who set this waterfall here as an eternal source of salmon for the people. For that is who came next: the salmon and the people. Below the falls, the river swells with tides. Above the falls, salmon nose their way to their birth waters. In the falls, salmon jump, sea lions bark, and the Clowwewalla people reach out their nets and are fed.

They call this place Charcowah. Magic Fish Trap.

THE PLACE WE MAKE

Chapter One

The Founder

Portrait of John McLoughlin, circa 1855.
Used by permission from the Minnesota Historical Society.

In 1829, a red-faced man with a shock of white hair and steel-blue eyes brought his vessel to rest at the base of a waterfall. Raised in Quebec by a Scotch Irish father and a French Canadian mother, the man had trained as a doctor before making his way across the continent as a fur trader. He was six feet, four inches tall and forty-five years old. A biographer would later gush that he was a "superb specimen of man" with "magnificent physical proportions." The Indigenous people called him "White-Headed Eagle." Others knew him as "the Czar of the West," whose "rule was imperial for a thousand miles." By the time of his voyage up the Willamette River that day, he was serving as chief factor of the Columbia region for the Hudson's Bay Company, supervising all British trade from Alaska to California, the Rockies to the Pacific. His name was John McLoughlin.

Did McLoughlin pause, just for a moment, to gaze in awe at the dense crowd of fir, maple, cedar, and oak trees that stood sentinel along the riverbanks? Did he stop to listen to the mighty rhythm pounded out by water jumping ceaselessly over rock? Did he notice the eyes—of elk, or deer, or Clowwewalla Indian—that might have peered out from among the trees, watching him? Or did he turn to his companion, George Simpson, and shout over the noise of the falls that they had reached the farthest inland point in the Willamette Valley accessible by ship? This was it. The end.

As they scrambled up the steep, grassy riverbank to the narrow strip of land running between the river and the nearby basalt cliffs, the men imagined a productive sawmill operating one day through the power of the waterfall. McLoughlin saw the place as a potential connection point between the fertile farmland south of the falls and the waterway north that would lead to trade with the outside world. He had found a site, he thought, "destined by nature to be the most important place in the country." He constructed three buildings there and "claimed land at Willamette Falls for England."

The story of North American land being claimed by the first White man to walk upon it stretches back, of course, to 1492. And that story held (among those who repeated it, anyway) for five hundred years—as late as 1999, John McLoughlin's biographer still conceived of the land McLoughlin found as "deep and rich, waiting for their plows." But the story of land lying in wait for White men's plows is not the first story told about this continent. Our First Nations have long told other stories. For them, the land is not a virgin to be conquered but a mother who freely offers what her children need. For them, the land's story does not begin with the first White footsteps. It stretches back, with the presence of their peoples, to the beginning of time.

"Almost every tribe," wrote Lakota activist and history professor Vine Deloria, Jr., "can point out those features of the landscape which mark the boundaries of their lands and tell how the people first knew that this was their country and that it was in exactly the right place."

The exact right place for the Clowwewalla people was the village they called Charcowah, with its most important feature: the mighty waterfall that provided them with fish. The ancestors of this small band of the Clackamas Tribe had fished and traded here for ten thousand years.

Just fifteen years before McLoughlin's visit, a Canadian explorer named Alexander Henry had passed by the Charcowah village, noting six longhouses and "numerous" Clowwewalla residents. But by the time McLoughlin arrived in 1829, waves of European diseases like smallpox and cholera had reduced the Clowwewalla numbers to a mere twenty-five to thirty inhabitants. Though few, they resisted McLoughlin's incursion by burning his three buildings to the ground.

McLoughlin had an intimate yet authoritarian relationship with the people indigenous to the territory he ruled. He took two Native wives in succession, the mothers of his five children. He believed in treating American Indians fairly and admonished his employees to do the same. Yet he was frustrated that an abundance of salmon and "Nutricious Roots" contributed to what he considered the Indians' "Lasiness," making them unwilling to work for him as often as he wished they would. McLoughlin also exacted swift punishment for perceived wrongs. When a Hudson's Bay employee was killed in an attempted robbery, McLoughlin pursued the Indigenous man alleged to be responsible for the crime and "made the arrangements for the execution in a way best calculated to strike terror to the Indian mind."

When the Clowwewalla burned his three buildings at Willamette Falls, McLoughlin rebuilt.

A town was born.

Seventeen years later, after the career that sent him roving up and down the West Coast came to an unfortunate end, McLoughlin returned to the falls of the Willamette. He was an older man now, approaching the end of his life. This time—disgraced by an ongoing feud with George Simpson that had cost him his job and disconsolate over the untimely death of his oldest son— McLoughlin came to stay.

In the intervening years since he'd first set foot there, McLoughlin had kept tabs on his claim. After erecting those first three buildings, he'd returned to his base at Fort Vancouver, twenty miles north, near the place where the Willamette River emptied into the

Columbia. But he'd left some company employees to mind the site at the base of the falls, and he had often returned to make improvements. In 1832, McLoughlin blasted a millrace. In 1838, he built a "house & store." In 1842, he platted the streets of his town and named it Oregon City. In 1844, he designated the location of Oregon City's jail. That same year, Oregon City became the first incorporated city west of the Rocky Mountains.

Shortly after, in 1846, McLoughlin moved to Oregon City permanently, with his second wife and a couple of adult children and their families, into a two-story house with a pyramid-shaped roof that he built with his own two hands. He opened a dry-goods store across the street. Depressed about his precipitous fall from chief factor of half a continent to proprietor of a small-town general store, McLoughlin sat in his new house in Oregon City and wrote to his former employer, "I have Drunk and am Drinking the cup of Bitterness to the very Dregs."

The house where McLoughlin drank his dregs was pictured on the cover of the New York City publication *Holden's Dollar Magazine* not long after the McLoughlins moved in—it is just to the right of the mast of the ship that lays at anchor, with the American flag pointing down at it. The sketch depicts the expansion of the town in its first two decades, far beyond its initial three buildings. As the first city in the West to be founded as a commercial center rather than as a military fort or religious mission, Oregon City's population had grown from a handful at the start of the decade to nine hundred at its close.

The sawmill McLoughlin had envisioned decades before is visible here in the etching, already humming. And McLoughlin's dream of ships streaming in from the Pacific has been realized too.

Etching of Oregon City, circa 1850. Library of Congress.

In the sketch, one ship stands ready for its supplies to be unloaded and portaged over Singer Creek, at the right edge of the picture, and past the Willamette Falls, which roars just outside the frame, to the waiting steamboats on the higher stage of the river. The other ship in the etching appears to be moving away from Oregon City, presumably full of exports produced by farmers in the fertile Willamette Valley. Still, for all this human activity, the town itself appears almost lost in the vast landscape of sun-tipped clouds, towering evergreens, soaring cliffs, and the glassy river. The artist has depicted the town's buildings as but a handful of dice scattered across the sliver of open land that hugs the river. To the *Holden's Dollar* readers in New York, the little town must have seemed awfully exotic and far away.

Oregon City was the focus of the national imagination just

then, toward the end of the 1840s. The closing decade had seen thousands of Americans toiling across the plains and over the Rockies, oxcarts laden with expectations. All their hopes were pinned on reaching those wooden structures scratched out between the bluffs and the river. Oregon City was the official End of the Oregon Trail. All over the country, from New York to Independence, Missouri, hearts were soaring at the very idea of Oregon City. Whatever the country would become—marching west in pursuit of her Manifest Destiny—she would become it in Oregon City.

The Library of Congress classifies the *Holden's Dollar Magazine* cover as the oldest known map of Oregon City, although it is not a map at all. It's easy to see why the inhabitants of the town would not yet have needed maps to navigate from house to house. No roads are visible, and the fifty-odd structures appear to be placed at random, eschewing the neat rows we moderns have come to associate with urban life. The two tiny groups of human-shaped figures sketched into the center of town would surely have known exactly who lived in which house.

Though maps were not yet necessary, flags were. The provenance of the territory had long been subject to dispute. Russia and Spain had withdrawn their claims to the region by the 1820s, but England and America continued to argue over their border in the West for another two decades. Although McLoughlin had originally claimed the land at Willamette Falls for England, he quickly recognized that the steady stream of Americans trooping across the continent would change the calculus. So while he was stationed at Fort Vancouver, McLoughlin provisioned the American settlers who straggled in and sent them south. He hoped that England might hold the land north of the Columbia River (present-day Washington State), leaving Oregon for America. Though McLoughlin's willingness to help the Americans earned him the wrath of his British employers, one hundred years after his death, it would earn him the title "Father of Oregon."

Just as McLoughlin had anticipated, the early Oregon settlers made it clear in their founding documents that their makeshift government was to stand only "until such time as the United States of America extend their jurisdiction over us." Official inclusion of the Oregon Territory into the holdings of the United States finally occurred in 1848. Perhaps it is in celebration or proclamation of this new arrangement that the artist sketched two different nineteenth-century versions of the American flag into the image. The Francis Hopkinson flag, its rows of stars neatly aligned in the upper left corner, streams from the top of a ship sailing out of view on the left edge of the picture. The Cowpens flag—with its circle of stars surrounding a single star in the field of blue—flies from the top of a double-masted schooner anchored in the harbor. Together, the flags declare the allegiance of the little village.

There is another symbol of the settlers' allegiance that stands in the center of town: its church steeple. Built in 1843, the Methodist Church in Oregon City was the first Protestant congregation established west of the Rocky Mountains. In the line drawing, the rooftops of the densest cluster of buildings rise to a triangular pinnacle apexed by the flag and the steeple. God and country—together they represent the twin loyalties of the town's people. The flag and steeple seem to announce that, from now on, this would be an American place and a Christian place.

What is *not* visible from the artist's rendering is the fact that, from its inception, this town was not just meant to be quintessentially Christian and American. It was also designed, legislated, and enforced to be a White utopia.

Throughout the 1840s and 1850s, as pioneers in covered wagons strained for months on end to reach McLoughlin's general store, where they could stake their claim to their own 160 acres of Oregon farmland, trouble was brewing behind them. The nation, of course, was headed for war. Even as the country rapidly expanded westward, mounting tensions threatened to tear it apart. And so, for every "free" state that became part of the Union in those years, Southern senators sought a slave state to go with it, so as not to upset the delicate balance of votes on the floor. Mississippi and Indiana came in together. Alabama and Illinois. Missouri and Maine. Which way would Oregon lean?

Today, we think of Oregon as a Northern state, a free state. At the time, however, the question of whether Oregon would enter the Union as a slave state was up for some discussion. Many of the settlers hailed from slave states like Missouri, and a few enslaved people did come across on the Oregon Trail with those who enslaved them. But most of the Oregon Trail pioneers weren't interested in enslaving others. By and large, they did not hail from the wealthy, slave-owning class of White people. If they had, they wouldn't have risked their lives on a team of oxen, a covered wagon, and a lengthy journey with an uncertain outcome. A deep economic depression had settled over the country in the 1840s, fostering the desperation that bred "Oregon Fever." Poor White Missourians looked at the seemingly endless supply of free labor then possessed by their slave-owning neighbors and felt that they could never keep up. "I'm going to Oregon," remarked one pioneer, "where there'll be no slaves, and we'll all start even." Oregon's provisional government voted to ban slavery in the Territory in 1843.

But opposition to slavery was not the same thing as hospitality toward Black people. Oregon settler Jesse Applegate wrote of his compatriots, "Many of those people hated slavery, but a much larger number of them hated free negroes worse even than slaves." Oregon pioneers viewed African Americans not as the help but as the competition—a competition they wanted to eliminate. Historians estimate the population of Black residents in the Oregon Territory in the 1840s at around fifteen. For some White settlers, it was fifteen too many.

Ambivalence about the slave issue they had left behind was not the only factor contributing to the settlers' mistrust. The pioneers were also uneasy about the world they had entered. When they reached Oregon, the settlers found themselves in a space that for centuries had already been populated by not only Indigenous tribes but also a multiethnic group of fur traders, missionaries, and sailors. A unique regional trade language ("Chinook wawa") comprised of a patois of Chinook, French, and English was widely spoken. Alliances had already been formed that the pioneers were not privy to. (Not that they desired alliances; they had come, as one said, "not to establish trade with the Indians, but to take and settle the country exclusively for [themselves].") Historian Kenneth Coleman wrote that when the settlers arrived in the Oregon

Territory, they "felt most vulnerable. Most had traveled incredible distances overland to arrive in an ethnically diverse region they did not fully understand." They sought to minimize their discomfort by maximizing the homogeneity of their new homeland.

One alliance, in particular, raised the settlers' apprehension. In 1844, a Black man named James Saules—a former sailor who had been living with a Chinook wife in the Willamette Valley for three years—aligned himself with the local tribe and, together with them, threatened violence against the White settler who had laid claim to their land. Saules said "he would stand for the Indians' rights" and that he was "armed and prepared to do so." He was arrested, tried, convicted, and placed in federal custody. After Saules was released, the federal agent who had detained him wrote to the United States secretary of war. "[Saules] ought to be transported, together with every other Negro, being in our condition dangerous subjects," the agent complained. "Until we have some further means of protection, their immigration ought to be prohibited. Can this be done?"

Evidently, it could. Mere weeks after the Saules case, Oregon's provisional government voted to amend the anti-slavery law it had passed the previous year. On June 26, 1844, the legislative council set a time limit of three years for Oregon's enslavers to remove their enslaved persons from the territory (effectively legalizing slavery in the state for the duration of those three years). At the end of that time, no Black person would be allowed to remain in Oregon. Anyone who refused to go would be punished by up to thirty-nine lashes with a whip every six months until the so-called criminal "quit the Territory."

There is no evidence that the "Lash Law" punishment was ever used. (There is no evidence that the prohibition against slavery was enforced either; Quintard Taylor estimated that between 1850 and 1860, "at least 14," and possibly as many as 135, enslaved people arrived in Oregon with their enslavers and were never informed of the fact that they should legally have been set free.) Under criticism that the proposed thirty-nine lashes was too harsh a punishment, Oregon's legislature repealed the Lash Law in 1845. But in 1849, they tried again. This time, the law stated that "any negro or mulatto" could not "enter into, or reside" in Oregon. This is the law that hangs invisibly over the houses and businesses on the cover of *Holden's Dollar Magazine*.

That law was rescinded in 1854. But three years later, at the constitutional convention organized in 1857 to prepare for statehood, Oregon legislators made a third attempt to exclude Black people from the state. They submitted two proposals to the convention's delegates: One, should Oregon enter the Union as a slave state? Two, should free Black residents be excluded? Delegates opposed the slavery proposal but approved the exclusion clause by a wide margin. Therefore, when Oregon's citizens ratified their new state's constitution, they approved a Bill of Rights that included Article 1, "We declare that all men, when they form a social compact are equal in right." But they also overwhelmingly approved this separate amendment: "No free Negro, or Mulatto, not residing in this state at the time of the adoption of this constitution, shall come, reside or be within this state." By granting "all men" equal rights, and in the same stroke denying equal rights to Black men, the state of Oregon began its official existence on the foundational premise that Black men were not men at all. The Exclusion Law was not repealed until 1926, by 62.5 percent of the vote.

For the first sixty-plus years of its existence, the state of Oregon banned Black people from even *being* within its borders. Towns where Black people were not welcome after dark were often called "sundown towns." As others have pointed out before me, Oregon was a sundown state. It was the only state in the United States of America ever to join the Union with an exclusion law on its books.

Peter Burnett, an influential pioneer who joined Oregon's first legislative body the year after he arrived and later became the first governor of California, is often called the father of the exclusion laws. He argued for that initial 1844 amendment by stating, "The object is to keep clear of that most troublesome class of population," by which he meant Black people. In a bitter and self-deluded twist of irony, Burnett saw his law as a means not of perpetuating evil but of avoiding it. "We are in a new world under the most favorable circumstances," he said, "and we wish to avoid most of those evils that have so much afflicted the United States and other countries." A 1916 historian explained that Burnett "was opposed to slavery largely on account of the evil to both the white and black races by the inevitable mixing of the races where slavery existed."

Burnett and his compatriots could not see that by trying to avoid "evil," they were reinforcing one of the gravest evils of them all.

I t is the summer of 1851. The second law preventing "any negro or mulatto" from entering or residing in the Oregon Territory is nearly two years old. A few more buildings have been constructed, perhaps, since the magazine cover picture was etched. The citizens of Oregon City have just elected their town's founder, Dr. John McLoughlin, as mayor. A new newspaper, the *Oregon Statesman*, has recently been established.

Reading the newspaper's notices and advertisements page feels like strolling through the commercial streets of the little town, hearing merchants calling out the day's bargains. In the June 6, 1851, edition of the *Statesman*, we read of the two competing surgeon dentists; of the prices of "butter, old" and "butter, fresh"; of lard, putty, soap, and sperm oil. Three dry-goods companies announce their plans to keep an assortment of merchandise "constantly on hand," while another mercantile, "being desirous of closing out their present stock," offers to exchange it for gold.

Does the young city already sense that the discovery of gold in California, just three years before, threatens their status as one of the most important commercial centers in the newly American West? The notices page is filled with gold: You can have it "insured and forwarded" by Adams & Co. or transported by the "superior facilities" of Todd & Co. Just about the only thing you can't do with gold in Oregon City is pull it out of the ground. The Klamath mines in southern Oregon, some 275 miles away, have optimistically taken out an advertisement. But if you can't find gold in Oregon, there is also an ad informing readers of the precise address of every church in San Francisco.

The times are mobile and transient. The steamship *Hoosier*, we read, "will run regularly between Oregon City and Dayton," a farming community some thirty miles upriver, carrying passengers and freight. But "the Keel Boat, Salem Clipper, still continues to run," another ad assures us. Two express companies promise to carry "packages of every description" to "all parts of the United States." Everyone and everything, it seems, is on the move.

With all this movement, some people have become lost altogether. "An afflicted mother," we find out, "will be greatly obliged by learning where her son, GEORGE RARITY, about 16 years, is." And there is a lost wallet—or a found wallet, rather: "much worn, containing some papers apparently belonging to Orville Krum," which the finder will return if said Mr. Krum will reimburse him for the cost of the advertisement. Two citizens of Oregon City have lately made their final journeys: Four-year-old Albert Johnson has died, as has thirty-one-year-old Ann Calhoun, leaving behind "a large family of small children," including an infant, one day old.

And then, in the third column of all this raucous humanity, five notices down, a small ad draws attention to itself with an ink drawing of a bird standing in the grass. "Oregon Saloon and Boarding House," the copy reads, "Main Street, opposite the Statesman Office. Meals furnished at the regular hours for 75 cents. Persons from the country are invited to call." At the bottom of the square, the proprietor of the establishment has signed his name.

It is the name of the only person in the history of the United States ever to be convicted and punished solely for the crime of being Black: Jacob Vanderpool.

We don't know much about Jacob Vanderpool, but his name alone holds a clue. Vanderpool: It's Dutch. A witness in the trial would testify that he believed Vanderpool came from the West Indies, which had been partially colonized by the Dutch. And court documents classified Vanderpool as "mulatto," or of mixed racial heritage. As a biracial man from the West Indies with the last name Vanderpool, it's highly likely that Jacob Vanderpool was descended from a male Dutch plantation owner and an enslaved African woman.

It was a consequential time for these two men, John McLoughlin and Jacob Vanderpool. Both had begun their lives outside the United States of America: Quebec for McLoughlin, the West Indies for Vanderpool. By the summer of 1851, both had made their way across the North American continent to Oregon City. The French Canadian was elected mayor in April. The Dutch African began advertising his boarding house in June. By the end of that short summer, John McLoughlin would be granted American citizenship. But Jacob Vanderpool would no longer have a business to advertise.

Chapter Two

From Ignorance to Empathy

[White people] are in effect still trapped in a history which they do not understand and until they understand it, they cannot be released from it.

—James Baldwin, "A Letter to My Nephew,"
The Progressive Magazine

I had no idea, when I moved into the house where I currently live, why the pawn-shop-and-car-lot-pocked highway at the end of my street was called McLoughlin Boulevard. I certainly had never heard of Jacob Vanderpool. I didn't know much about Oregon at all. I'd grown up visiting my paternal grandparents in Corvallis, the home of Oregon State University. I was even born in Portland, in the hospital where my father was completing his medical school training. But we'd moved out of the state when I was two, and for most of my life, I'd lived elsewhere. So when I returned to live here as an adult, it was both a homecoming and a journey into the unknown.

Of Oregon City, in particular, I knew practically nothing. I am a member of what's sometimes called the Oregon Trail Generation: the "microgeneration" born between 1977 and 1985 who grew up playing the *Oregon Trail* video game prepackaged onto early Apple computers. As I sat in my sixth-grade classroom outside Boston, Massachusetts, repeatedly pressing the space bar to fire square bullets at blocky buffalo, I had only a vague notion of Oregon City as a digital wonderland my avatar could almost never reach for lack of food or the intrusion of disease: You Have Died of Dysentery. I'm not even sure I knew it was a real town. I certainly had no idea that some of my own distant relatives had once traveled the non-pixelated version of the Oregon Trail. My great-great-great-grandfather's brother, Lyman D. C. Latourette, had come across the Great Plains in an oxcart in 1848 and lived in Oregon City for the rest of his life. Many of his descendants—my fourth cousins, if I'm reading the cousin chart correctly—still live here.

When I moved next door to Oregon City as an adult, I knew the historic town merely as a good place to rent my kids' band instruments or grab a slice of pizza. Later, I knew it as my place of employment: I got a job teaching in one of the oldest school buildings in Oregon City and passed the sign proclaiming "The End of the Oregon Trail" every morning as I drove to work. But I had no idea, strolling along the ridge above downtown with my husband and four children, that when I recognized my maternal grandmother's maiden name painted over the doorways of some of the grandest old Victorian homes, it was because those homes had once belonged to my own family members. I had no idea that my own great-great-great-grandmother had come to Oregon City to live with relatives before she died and was buried right here in the Mountain View Cemetery. Or that D.C. Latourette Park, on Monroe Street, was named for one of my cousins. I had no idea that members of my family had once been Oregon's mayors, schoolteachers, pastors, judges, and state legislators. Whatever this town had become, whatever this state had become, my own flesh and blood had a hand in building it.

Still, for all I didn't know, there *were* things I noticed about Oregon right away. One of the first observations that struck me was that I was surrounded by White people. The year after we moved to the suburb twenty minutes outside Portland, *The Atlantic* called it "the Whitest City in America." One of my new colleagues told me that, growing up in rural Oregon, she'd never even *seen* a Black person until high school. When I first moved here, I could go for days—sometimes even weeks—visiting all the usual spaces of my ordinary routine without seeing any people of color at all.

Granted, most of the institutions, schools, churches, and neighborhoods I had lived in before moving to the "End of the Oregon Trail" had also been populated mostly by White people like me. But there were always people of color around *somewhere*, enough to lull me into the false sense that our vast multicultural and supposedly post-racial society was running smoothly. So what if there weren't any Black kids in the "gifted and talented" elementary school classes I'd attended? There were Black kids in the rooms on the other side of the hall. So what if the churches my husband had pastored were mostly filled with White congregants? There were churches for communities of color just across town. Everything was fine. Everyone was humming along, happy in the places they'd made for themselves. Weren't they?

Then I moved to Oregon. The Whiteness slapped me in the face. Was this how it was supposed to be?

While the recognition startled me, at first I didn't wonder much about the reason an entire state was low on melanin. We just happened to be a long way, I supposed, from the Southern states where plantation owners had forced those first Africans to begin their American lives. Black Americans just . . . hadn't gotten here yet. Right?

I was even rather proud of myself for noticing the situation in the first place. What a keen observational eye I had. So, *of course*, I brought it up in the first conversation I had with a Black person after moving to Oregon.

My fifth-grade daughter, Abby, and I were in line for admittance to a concert three weeks after our move. We'd basically dragged our oldest child kicking and screaming over the state line to her new home, and these tickets had been purchased months before as a kind of appeasement. *Oh look! Your favorite Christian pop star is playing in Oregon right after we get there! Oregon can't be all bad!*

The line to get into the church that evening was populated with a smattering of the first Black people I'd seen since moving here. One woman was in line just in front of us. During our long wait, she turned around and we started talking. She worked at her church; my husband is a pastor. She was accompanied by her tween daughter; so was I. We both lived in Oregon. We settled into the easy banter of moms with a few things in common.

I don't remember how the conversation landed in a place where I even thought to utter my next words, but I distinctly remember saying them.

"Well, you know," I said, "there aren't very many Black people in Oregon."

She stared at me. I stared at her. My words hung between us. I had the sense to know I'd said something wrong, but I couldn't quite figure out what it was. Weren't my words true? Wasn't my bringing them up at all a sort of advocacy, a declaration that I was an ally, an astute enough observer that I, with my three-week-long residency in the state of Oregon, was ready to make pronouncements?

Apparently not. My new acquaintance jostled herself into a different spot, farther back in line, leaving me to chat with the White mom who now stood directly in front of me.

The best I could work out—although, admittedly, this working out took months—was that I'd committed a kind of Whitesplaining. *How would you feel*, I asked myself, *if you were in a space that was mostly men and one of them stood right in front of you and said, "I don't know if you've noticed, but there aren't very many women around here!"?* Once I'd managed to land there, I bit my lip in shame.

There was so much I didn't know.

Author Layla Saad wrote that when White people ask her what they should do about White supremacy, she responds with a question: "How have you managed not to know?" That question has been reverberating in me ever since I read it. How had I managed not to know what to do about White supremacy? How had I managed not to know that White supremacy was a problem in the first place? How had I managed not to know that the origin story of Oregon's Whiteness would be a sinister one? How had I managed not to know that bringing it up with the first Black person I saw in the state of Oregon might not end well?

The version of American history I learned in school might best be called American History Lite (or, perhaps, American History: White). The entirety of all necessary facts I remembered from my public school education about the history of racism in America could be summed up in two statements:

1. In 1865, Abraham Lincoln ended the slavery problem.

2. In the 1960s, Martin Luther King, Jr., ended the segregation problem.

End of story. Not a word about police brutality or redlining or school-to-prison pipelines or any of the myriad ways that our society, for any progress that has been made, remains a racialized one. Not a word about the burden our society imposes on Black people at nearly every level of social life. Not a word about racism perpetrated anywhere outside the Deep South or toward other communities of color (except perhaps a brief mention of the Trail of Tears). I remember, instead, an activity in which our teachers concocted an elaborate pudding taste test in the cafeteria— *Surprise! The cream-colored pudding tastes like chocolate and the brown pudding tastes like vanilla!*—which was somehow supposed to encourage us to be friends with everyone, and that was the sum of it.

But the fact was, even though no one had ever said a word about it, I had been moving in and out of historically segregated spaces my entire life. They were just small enough and fitted cleverly enough into the larger society that I hadn't seen them for what they were. One did not need to ask too many probing questions. Those mostly White gifted-and-talented classrooms? Those mostly White churches? Who made them? How did they become what they were? Of course, many factors influence the choices each individual makes today about where to worship God and how to educate their children, but there is also a well-documented history of racial segregation in schools and churches that I'd somehow managed not to think much about. It wasn't until I found myself in a historically segregated space 360 miles long and 400 miles wide that I sat up and blinked.

Still, I wouldn't have understood if my brother hadn't told me. Eleven years my junior and the graduate of a far more progressive college than the one I'd attended, Joe had a ready answer when I informed him of the Mystery of the Great White State.

"You didn't know?" He scowled at me, incredulous. "Oregon had an exclusion law that prohibited Black people from living there."

"What?!" It was my turn with the incredulous scowl.

This is a familiar response, yes? The jaw drop of incredulity every time we learn about something terrible that White people have done to people of color? Watch the video of Derek Chauvin kneeling on the neck of George Floyd—*What?!* Read Ibram X. Kendi explain the taxonomy of humanity concocted by Swedish botanist

Carl Linnaeus in 1735, from the "vigorous, muscular" *Homo sapiens europaeus* to the "sluggish, lazy" *Homo sapiens afer—What?!* Listen to a friend's story about the racist comment a grown adult made to her when she was only nine—*What?!*

How have we White people managed to be so shocked by White supremacy every single time? What is this cloak we draw, again and again, over our own eyes?

It's a defense mechanism, of course. We cannot solely blame our educational systems for our ignorance. Whatever lived in our teachers and our textbook writers, compelling them to gloss over so much horror, lives also in us. Confronting our own racism is too much; it's too hard. It's easier to allow ourselves to be shocked, again and again, than to admit we might have known all along. The dropped jaw says, "I didn't know about this!"—a necessary stepping stone to "It can't be my fault." Because if we might have known, if we might have been complicit, if the racism *out there* on White nationalist websites and Ku Klux Klan rallies might possibly have anything to do with what goes on *in here*, in the inner workings of our own subconscious—well, what would we do with *that*?

Confronting racism is emotionally challenging work. It's easier to hold it at arm's length, to pretend it is someone else's problem. Repeated shock is easier than sustained sorrow.

But reckoning with racism is a sorrowful business. We have much to grieve. And the first step that opened itself before me was to begin to imagine what it would be like *not* to be shocked by racism. The first step I took was to enter imaginatively and humbly—

with ears, eyes, and heart wide open—into the stories people of color had been telling all along.

The first time I read Richard Wright's 1937 essay "The Ethics of Living Jim Crow: An Autobiographical Sketch," it took my breath away. I stumbled across it while flipping through a fat volume I'd checked out from the library, *The Best American Essays of the Century.* When I read Wright's words, I realized that for my entire life, I had been getting the Jim Crow era entirely wrong.

I'd always thought it was about the water fountains. That's how it was presented in school: *They made them use different water fountains! Isn't that awful?* But to my prepubescent ears, it didn't sound particularly awful. At that stage of my life, I was used to being told exactly which utilities were available to me and which were not. The bathrooms on the back hallway were for fifth graders. The "lounge" behind the main office was for teachers. Girls used this bathroom; boys used that one. Segregation made a certain kind of elementary-school sense. Everybody got a drink of water, didn't they? What was the big deal? Of course, I nodded and played along—*Oh, yes, sitting in the back of the bus would be terrible*—but I was confused, because everybody in my world knew that the cool kids *loved* the back of the bus. Jim Crow, apparently, whoever he was, had made Black people sit where only cool kids were allowed to sit today. That was my elementary-level understanding, and it didn't mature very much until I got to the fourth decade of my life.

Then I read Richard Wright. And I realized that the core evil of the Jim Crow era was not the water fountains; it was the hate.

The Jim Crow world into which Wright dropped his readers, through the eyes of his young Black narrator, was violent, unpredictable, and terrifying. When the "quite small" Wright and his friends got into a cinder-block-and-broken-glass battle with a gang of White children, Wright's mother beat him until he had a fever of 102. She was trying to make him learn, trying to prevent more violence from coming to him. But avoiding violence as a young Black man in a White world proved impossible. Wright got a whiskey bottle to the face for forgetting to say "sir." He watched his boss drag, kick, and beat a Black woman who could not pay her bill. He got stopped and searched by police for making deliveries for his employer in a White neighborhood after sundown.

But worse than the violence were the threats of more violence. Every brush with White rage ended with a terrifying premonition that the full measure of racialized rage had not yet been meted out. When Wright forgot to use "Mr." when addressing his White co-worker, the co-worker forced Wright to walk away from the job and never return or "I'll rip yo' string gut loose with this bar!" When Wright told the story of the beaten non-bill-paying woman to his friends, they marveled, "It's a wonder they didn't lay her when they got through." The men who smashed the whiskey bottle to his face left him with the words "If yuh'd said tha' t' somebody else, yuh might've been . . . dead." When a fellow bellboy was *castrated* for sleeping with a White prostitute, the other bellboys were told that he was "mighty, mighty lucky"; if they tried the same trick, they likely wouldn't escape with their lives. Each time a White person lashed out violently, they followed up their violence with the threat of more.

Not once in the essay did Wright mention how sad it was to use a different water fountain. He did long for a house with a patch of grass and a job that required some shred of his intellect. But the true horror of the lived reality of Jim Crow was not the physical circumstances themselves; it was the living, breathing terror of having to encounter, again and again, the White *people* who made it their life's work to keep the Black populace stuck in those circumstances.

This is what we did *not* learn in my schools. We focused on the sentimental, more palatable effects of racism, those best poised to sketch the general shape without too many uncomfortable questions later at the dinner table: the hand-me-down, outdated school textbooks; the separate entrances; the back of the bus. We never looked the racists themselves in the eye.

It was the people, with their astonishing capacity for violence and evil—and then, too, it was all those other White people who did not exercise violence themselves but who had an astonishing capacity to simply keep walking—who made the Jim Crow era so unspeakably inhumane. And I never knew. I never knew.

We don't know what we don't allow ourselves to know. But when I began to know—after I'd picked my jaw up off the floor enough times to wonder if maybe there was a pattern to the small, individual shocks I kept receiving—the first dimension of my own racism that God called me to turn from was the sin of not knowing. Ignorance is not always sinful; there is no moral obligation to remember the Pythagorean theorem or the vice president's birthday (unless, perhaps, you are a structural engineer or the vice president's spouse). But to spend decades living in a society that has been obviously shaped along racialized lines and never to allow the injustices around me to nudge me toward curiosity? That was a sin, not of commission but of omission.

But the opposite of ignorance is not mere knowledge. Just as harmful as not knowing was using a little bit of knowledge to make myself seem smarter. *Well, you know, there aren't very many Black people in Oregon!* What I needed—in that conversation with the mom at the concert and in the rest of my life—was not so much knowledge as empathy.

Empathy: the discipline of encountering another person's story and allowing ourselves to imagine our own way in. Beginning with Richard Wright, the first place where I began to exchange ignorance for empathy was on the page. The page was a safe space to learn to listen to other people's stories. From my mostly White suburb of the Whitest city in America, I did not have immediate access to many relationships with people of color. What I had was the public library.

When it finally dawned on me that I had not been given the tools I needed to understand the world in which I lived, the first thing I did was read. I read memoirs by living authors of color— Austin Channing Brown, Marjane Satrapi, Charles M. Blow, Nicole Chung, Sherman Alexie, Richard Rodriguez, Jesmyn Ward; and those who had died—Frederick Douglass, James Baldwin, Maya Angelou. I read books by journalists like Ta-Nehisi Coates and Ruby Hamad; activists like Ijeoma Oluo and Heather McGhee; historians like Ibram X. Kendi, Isabel Wilkerson, and Jemar Tisby; theologians like Willie James Jennings, Chanequa Walker-Barnes, Esau McCaulley, Mark Charles, and Soong-Chan Rah. I read fiction by Louise Erdrich and Khaled Hosseini and Zadie Smith and Jamaica Kincaid. I read the poetry of Lucille Clifton and Phillis Wheatley and Naomi Shihab Nye and Claudia Rankine and Langston Hughes. I read widely and quixotically. I read what friends recommended and what I saw on social media and what I bumped into at the bookstore. It was as if I were making up for a lifetime of thirst by flinging my whole body into a rushing river and opening my mouth. As I read, I could almost feel my soul expanding, as though the words were pushing at my edges, forcing me to make room.

I read online too. Among other things, I spent time tracking down articles about the history of Oregon. I wanted to understand who had made the place where I lived, and how, and why. I didn't begin with Oregon because it was worse than any other place; I began with Oregon simply because it was *my* place. And it was on one of those websites that the name Jacob Vanderpool first shimmered out at me.

My friend Velynn Brown describes the moment when something in the world calls out to you as a "soul snag." It is the experience Moses had at the burning bush—the double take when some word or object says, *Look again.* That is what happened to me when I first saw his name, in the middle of an ordinary sentence on an ordinary web page.

"In 1851, Jacob Vanderpool, the black owner of a saloon, restaurant and boarding home, was actually expelled from the Oregon territory."

His name wasn't highlighted on the page, but it might as well have been for the way it leaped out at me.

Jacob Vanderpool.

To this day, I can't explain why it hooked me. He was Black; I was White. He was male; I was female. He was dead, an artifact of history; I was alive and very much a member of the modern age. But we had this in common: Each of us was one human being, whole yet small. And each of us had stood *here*—with all the uniqueness and yet relative insignificance of our respective lives—on Oregon soil.

What else might there be to find out about us?

Chapter Three

The Treasure Hunter

Portrait of Theophilus Magruder, circa 1856.
Used by permission from the Del Norte County Historical Society.

S cant clues dot the trail that traces from the West Indies plantation where Jacob Vanderpool probably began his life to the
boarding house in Oregon City where another chapter so firmly
closed. We do know that Vanderpool's presumably light-brown
skin—what Caroline Randall Williams called "rape-colored

skin"—would not have been an unusual sight in his homeland. By the 1800s, colonizers in the West Indies had developed an elaborate social system of condoning sexual relations with Black and so-called mulatto women. Some of the children of those unions were free, not enslaved, and had been so for generations. Still, they faced "intense discrimination, few job opportunities, and virtually no educational options." It's not surprising that the young Vanderpool would have left the land of his birth seeking another place to call home.

We know from court documents that before he opened his boarding house, Vanderpool worked as a sailor—a natural choice for a young man born on an island, an instant portal to other worlds. His racial heritage would not have been atypical here either. In the nineteenth century, Black sailors made up 20 percent of American ships' crews.

We also know that Vanderpool did not sail directly from the West Indies to Oregon. The 1850 United States Census puts Jacob Vanderpool—a free Black man, age thirty, birthplace West Indies, occupation seaman—at home in New York City. Here, too, he was not alone. The census records a wife, Eliza, and three children, all born free in the state of New York: twin three-year-olds, Jane and Amelia, and a newborn baby, Martin.

But was Jacob at home in New York on that July day when the census taker came knocking, or did Eliza merely provide information on her husband's behalf while he was away? A trial witness would report that Vanderpool had arrived in Oregon City in August 1850. If that's true, then he must have embarked on the eight-month journey around Cape Horn by January. This means that when Jacob Vanderpool set sail from New York—perhaps already

and also reckless . . . vociferous and very profane." That writer moved his things out of the City Hotel the very next day. It's not clear how long Magruder attempted to run that hotel. But just a few years later—with another establishment that, while it can't have been very old, already stood in need of "thorough repair," perhaps of both its structure and its reputation—he was trying again.

Vanderpool had continued to run his ad weekly, starting from that first advertisement in June. In the July 8 edition of the paper, Theophilus Magruder's first notice stands just four columns from Vanderpool's regular ad. The two men were attempting to establish themselves as hotel operators in that same small city during the summer of 1851. And, apparently, it didn't take Theophilus Magruder long to realize that the Black exclusion law could be a handy means of eliminating his competition.

On July 15, a week after Theophilus Magruder's notice first appeared in the *Statesman*, Jacob Vanderpool's ad did not run. It was the only week that summer that Vanderpool's ad went missing. I wondered why Vanderpool's ad had skipped that particular week. Had Magruder threatened Vanderpool with violence if his advertisements continued? Or had Magruder convinced a crony at the newspaper to make a certain competitor's notice go missing? Maybe Vanderpool's missed week had nothing to do with Theophilus Magruder. There were a million possible scenarios, and I had no way of knowing. All I had were the ads in the paper: On June 6, Vanderpool began running his ads weekly. On July 8, Magruder's weekly notice first appeared. On July 15, Vanderpool's ad was gone.

Then, on July 22, Vanderpool's ad reappeared. And less than a month later, Magruder would find a new way to threaten him.

The life Jacob Vanderpool led before coming to Oregon City remained, for me, only in hints and shadows. Theophilus Magruder's life, on the other hand, was eminently traceable. His name alone helped. The first name was unusual enough to my modern ears. Meaning "loved by God," it was the namesake of the biblical "most excellent Theophilus," to whom the apostle Luke wrote both his gospel and the book of Acts. But taken together with the last name, Oregon City's Theophilus Magruder appeared to be the only Theophilus Magruder the world had ever known. Every hit I could find led back to the same man—born 1799, died 1886. And he was everywhere. A celebrated pioneer and a child of privilege, Magruder enjoyed a wide variety of historical mentions far beyond his role in the Jacob Vanderpool case. And all of them painted a picture of a man driven by greed.

Born at the turn of the nineteenth century on the site where the National Capitol stands today, Theophilus Magruder was brought up with the country. His father, Patrick Magruder, served a term as a United States congressman before President Thomas Jefferson appointed him the second-ever Librarian of Congress, a post that at the time also included responsibilities as the clerk of the House of Representatives. Patrick and his wife Martha were D.C. elites and socialites, friends of President James Madison. Coming up in that milieu, young Theophilus might have assumed that he, too, was bound for greatness.

But when Theophilus was only sixteen, his father resigned from his post. Congress had opened an investigation into the elder Magruder's use of library funds for personal expenditures. More than a quarter of a million dollars, in today's money, had gone missing. Theophilus's stepmother died the following year (his mother had died when he was four), and his father passed away just two years later. Just as he was coming of age, Magruder became an orphan. Perhaps because of his father's disgraced status, Theophilus was unable to find his footing in the nation's capital. For a while, he disappears from the historical record.

Then, in 1844, Magruder resurfaced in Illinois: a married, middle-aged father of four. There, he and his friend James Marshall hatched a plan to travel the newly forged Oregon Trail. Their aim in going west was to search for gold. As a child, Magruder had seen gold nuggets on display in Washington, D.C., and was mesmerized by them.

The two friends set out together, but upon arrival in Oregon, they decided to split up. Magruder stayed behind in Oregon City, while Marshall struck out for California. In 1848, James Marshall himself found the very first gold flakes that sparked the California Gold Rush. As the California miners poured back into Oregon with a combined total of more than two million dollars' worth of gold—according to one eyewitness, there were "thousands of dollars' worth of gold dust" on every Oregon gambling table—Magruder might have bitterly regretted his choice.

Though he did not find gold in Oregon, Theophilus Magruder did manage to obtain the positions of power in the young American West that had eluded him in the nation's capital. In 1845,

Magruder served on the Oregon provisional legislature, the same group that had passed the first Black exclusion law just the year before. In fact, the legislative body met at Magruder's house, and they appointed him sergeant-at-arms. Magruder also served, for one month in 1849, as the Territory of Oregon's first secretary of state.

And he made money—literally. Theophilus Magruder joined a group of men who organized the minting of a new Oregon currency, which they called "Beaver Money." The five-dollar coins were pressed with *K.M.T.A.W.R.G.S.*, one letter for each founder's initial. The *M* stands for Magruder. The currency was declared illegal by Oregon's first territory governor, Joseph Lane, and the group disbanded before they could ever turn a profit.*

Although he took such extraordinary steps to clear the field of competition for his Main Street Hotel, Magruder did not stay long in Oregon City after the Vanderpool trial. In 1854, he and his family followed their sixteen-year-old daughter to Crescent City, California, where she married a twenty-seven-year-old lumber tycoon named Joseph Wall. Perhaps Magruder hoped that by marrying his teenage daughter off to a wealthy man, some status would accrue to him. According to her obituary, Margaret Wall died "one of California's wealthiest and most popular pioneer women." But "wealthiest" and "most popular" were not superlatives that anyone seems to have ever applied to her father.

Magruder was certainly not popular with the American Indians for whom he was briefly responsible. In 1855, Magruder was ap-

---

*Today, one of those five-dollar coins is worth twenty-seven thousand dollars.

pointed to run an internment camp filled with hundreds of "Umpqua, Calapooia, Cow, Creek, and Molalla Indians." Many of the prisoners under Magruder's care were not well. A visitor noted that many were "suffering . . . probably induced by a change of diet . . . and exposure" to eleven inches of snow. The visitor personally purchased, for the people in the camp, supplies that Magruder had not bothered to provide. Eventually, those who survived Magruder's prison were moved to a reservation.

Theophilus Magruder's last recorded grasp at lucrative work earned him a place in the annals of avid lighthouse historians. But even this relatively straightforward position was not without complications. In 1856, Magruder took a post as the first lighthouse keeper of the Battery Point Lighthouse in Crescent City, California. But he arrived two weeks late for the job, forcing the lighthouse board to scramble for a temporary keeper. He quit less than three years later when the board voted to reduce his salary.

Theophilus Magruder died in Crescent City at the age of eighty-seven.

The orphaned son of a man who died while under congressional investigation for embezzlement. Onetime friend and travel partner of the man who started the California Gold Rush. Founder of a scotched attempt at minting illegal currency. Operator of a series of rowdy hotels. Father of a teenage bride married off to a lumber magnate. Neglectful American Indian prison warden. Disgruntled lighthouse employee. Time and again, Theophilus Magruder comes close but cannot quite seem to grasp the riches he seeks. Is it any wonder that this man also appears as the plaintiff in a case whose outcome would be the exile of one of his main business competitors?

But to truly understand the racial animus behind Magruder's lawsuit—the ease with which he reads Jacob Vanderpool, specifically, as expendable—we must return to his parents' ancestral home. Theophilus's mother had died when he was only four, and his father remarried when he was twelve. The Virginia farm where his stepmother had grown up was known as "Sweden." Theophilus's father retired there after his resignation. The disgraced former congressman died and was buried there, as was his second wife. Young Theophilus himself must have spent many a day there.

It was a large slave-owning plantation.

They did not plan to set up a vast empire of enslavement, those first English colonists who arrived in the New World. Virginian colonists purchased African slaves as early as 1619, but the practice of race-based chattel slavery did not gain immediate and widespread traction. Historian Edmund S. Morgan noted that the colonists "did not import shiploads of African slaves to solve their labor problem until half a century more had passed." In his book *American Slavery, American Freedom*, Morgan showed that throughout most of the seventeenth century, English colonists found a ready supply of labor via the same system used for centuries by their compatriots in England: indentured servitude. Unemployment rates were high in England, and the need for help was great in the colonies. As a result, most of the workers in the early American colonies were White and English, just like their employers. They came over on ships from England, paid for their passage with five to seven years of hard work, and then joined the ranks of the free.

This system worked fine in the beginning, especially in the first few decades of colonization, when the pressures of a new climate, with its new diseases and unfamiliar agricultural practices, resulted in exceptionally high mortality rates. Indentured servants frequently died before their time of service was complete, which didn't matter to their employers because there were always more boatloads of potential laborers coming after them. But after half a century or so, as the American colonists adapted to their new country, more indentured servants began living through to the end of their terms of service. This meant that with each "graduating class" of servants whose indenture was complete, there were more free White men and women eager to join the established society. And that meant more competition in the fledgling economy their society was attempting to sustain. The supreme flaw of indentured servitude, wrote Morgan, was that "every year it poured a host of new freemen into a society where the opportunities for advancement were limited."

A protracted struggle ensued between the emerging lower class of the White former servants and the emerging upper class of the more established White landowners. All of them had come to the New World to seek their fortunes. The problem was that the East Coast of America did not yield the fortunes any of them had expected. There were no spices, no silks, no silver, no gold. The only export the early colonists could reliably produce (before the invention of the cotton gin) was tobacco. But tobacco prices had recently precipitously dropped. The landowners realized that if they allowed their former servants to set up shop as tobacco farmers, pumping more and more of the land's only cash crop into the market, the result would be less money for everybody. So rather than allow the newly freed servants to lay claim to some of the seemingly limitless land that the landowners themselves had simply walked in and taken decades before, the landowners scrambled to extend their dominion over as much land as possible. As a result, much potentially arable land remained fallow and forested; on paper, it was owned by a small number of wealthy men. If the newly freed servants wanted to work the soil, they could rent it.

Seeking to solidify control over the working class, the landowners implemented an ever more elaborate system of taxes, punishments, and fees. As the newly freed servants saw that the game was rigged against them, they responded with a series of increasingly well-organized rebellions.

Amid this conflict, the landowners began to realize that their problems could be solved if only they could stop releasing so many newly freed people into their society. That meant bringing fewer indentured servants into the colonies in the first place. Workers who would never be freed fit the bill nicely. Gradually, over the second half of the seventeenth century, the landowners stopped accepting English servants and instead began purchasing enslaved people from the West Indies, where a bustling commerce in slavery had already been established. "These were the men who brought slavery to Virginia"—and, by extension, to America— wrote Morgan, "simply by buying slaves instead of servants."

American slavery was not established through an expansive set of laws or a single powerful leader or a grand macabre plan. It began, rather, as a series of business decisions made by individual plantation owners—men who had come to America to get rich and could not abide the thought that other men might try to come to America to get rich too. Just as Theophilus Magruder sought to minimize competition by eliminating Jacob Vanderpool from Oregon City, his great-grandparents had sought to minimize competition by eliminating White indentured servants from the colonies. They'd turned instead to slavery, a system that would remain in place for hundreds of years, stealing the lives and livelihoods of ten million enslaved Black Americans and requiring the deaths of 750,000 American soldiers—Black, White, Asian, Hispanic, and American Indian—in the Civil War to bring it to its legal end.

Edmund Morgan focused his story on Virginia, the oldest of the American colonies and the locus of the systematization of American slavery. But slavery did not merely spread from Virginia to the rest of the South. It existed in all thirteen of the original American colonies. And even after slavery was outlawed in the North, the entire country remained economically united around slavery's profits.

Maintaining slavery was even one of the motives of the American revolutionaries. The famous patriot Samuel Adams wrote an early revolutionary screed warning that among all the outrageous acts committed by the British soldiers then quartering in Boston, "the most atrocious offense and alarming behavior" was that of a British captain who attempted to "excite an insurrection" by persuading some African slaves that "the soldiers were come to procure their freedom." It is notable that the *worst* offense of the British soldiers, in Adams's eyes, was to tell American slaves that they might be free. The American Revolution was fought, in part, to preserve the institution of slavery.

The country that incubated the idea that "all men are created equal" had simultaneously nurtured a system of notorious inequality. President Thomas Jefferson himself, who was at the same time the author of those famous words about equality, and the owner—and father—of numerous enslaved people, knew the tension inherent in the American system. As Jefferson noted,

> The whole commerce between master and slave is a perpetual exercise of . . . the most unremitting despotism on the one part, and degrading submissions on the other. Our children see this, and learn to imitate it. . . .
> The parent storms, the child looks on, catches the lineaments of wrath, puts on the same airs in the circle of smaller slaves, gives a loose to his worst of passions, and thus nursed, educated, and daily exercised in tyranny, cannot but be stamped by it.

Our children see this and learn to imitate it. That was exactly what had happened with Theophilus Magruder. He'd come of age in Virginia, the cradle of American slavery. He'd seen from his earliest years that Black people existed to fulfill his whims. So it's no wonder that after he arrived in Oregon, Magruder viewed Jacob Vanderpool merely as a pawn in his game, someone to be moved aside as profits demanded.

Theophilus Magruder was simply reenacting the tyranny in which he had been nursed, educated, and daily exercised.

❧

So much is lost to us as we peer back through time from our distant vantage point. Did Theophilus Magruder work up a backroom deal with other powerful townsmen, or did he come up with the idea for the lawsuit on his own? Did the sheriff arrest Jacob Vanderpool quietly, after hours, or did he handcuff him while Vanderpool was in the middle of serving customers and lead him away? Had Magruder and Vanderpool ever exchanged words before, in one or the other of their establishments or out on the street? What flashed between them—or didn't—when they met there in that courtroom?

The only thing we know is what we have in the court documents.

The first document records that on August 20, 1851, Theophilus Magruder appeared before the Supreme Court of the Territory of Oregon to make a formal complaint. There, he "saith," the court transcript records, "that one Jacob Vanderpool, a mulatto, for more than forty days has resided and now resides in Oregon City." He stated that he believed he could prove Vanderpool had arrived in Oregon after September 26, 1849. That was the date when the most recent exclusion law had gone into effect; any Black people living in Oregon prior to that date had been grandfathered in. Magruder ended with a simple appeal: He "prays that a warrant may open for the arrest of the said Jacob Vanderpool and that he is dealt with according to law."

Magruder *prayed* for Vanderpool's arrest. It was only old-fashioned language for making a petition, I knew, but it struck me as deeply ironic that in his plot to miscarry justice, Magruder would even hint at the involvement of God.

That night, as the *Statesman* would later report, Oregon City endured the most ferocious rainstorm its residents had ever seen.

The next day, Jacob Vanderpool was in custody.

Chapter Four

From Clenched Fists
to Open Hands

We are writing from the vantage of those who owe reparations and who have benefited from the thefts of White supremacy. We believe that our role is to tell the truth about this theft, to own the complex ways in which we are implicated in it, and to struggle toward the work of repair.

—Duke L. Kwon and Gregory Thompson, *Reparations*

W hen I first began researching, every reference I found dispatched Jacob Vanderpool in a sentence or two: the law, the hotel, the trial, the expulsion.

But there was a single primary source. The Special Collections Library of the University of Oregon in Eugene held a folder of court documents from the 1851 proceedings. Eugene was two hours from my house, so I emailed the library to see if they could send me copies. They promptly responded that they were happy to do so; the fee for the service was fifty dollars. But fifty dollars was a lot of money. I let the email sit in my inbox.

There was another historical document I wanted to track down.

One that should have been easier to find. It was a piece of paper my father had once sent me in the mail, a photocopy of an old family will. I remembered the block of dense ink running down the center of the page: a handwritten list of property that one of my direct ancestors was leaving, upon his death, to the next ancestor down.

Some of the entries on that list were human beings.

All I knew of my mother's side of the family were the Latourettes, Protestant Huguenots who had fled religious persecution in France, bouncing around the northern half of the United States for several generations—New York, Wisconsin, Indiana—before packing up their oxcarts and trundling west. But on my father's side, the Williams family, in their pre-Oregon days, had hailed from Kentucky. As a child, I'd visited Pine Knot, where my father's mother was raised—the one-stop-sign town where my father taught me to lay pennies on the railroad tracks in anticipation of a coming train. And I'd been to Springfield, where my father's father had worked in his father's drugstore. It was one of the father's father's fathers in that line who'd made out the will my own father had sent to me.

I'd stared at it for a while. We'd had a phone conversation about it shortly after it arrived in the mail. "Did you notice the names in the will?" my father had asked. "That's proof that one of our ancestors owned slaves."

He said this with the utmost nonchalance, as if asking whether I'd noticed that the price of milk had dropped by two cents a gallon or that there was a tiny stain on the elbow of my oldest sweater. When I later read of Wendell Berry telling how his own Kentucky relatives had "casually" passed down their family's stories of slaveholding, using the word *casually* three times in as many sentences, I knew exactly what he meant.

And then, I had casually lost my family's list. Maybe I had thrown it away. Maybe I decided that I didn't want to hold on to that particular piece of paper. Maybe I decided that my family's enslavement of other families was not something I wanted to be able to prove. I don't remember. All I knew was that now, when I turned my haphazard filing system upside down and pawed through every page, the photocopy was gone.

This losing, this forgetting, this refusing to look had felt so inconsequential to me at the time—of course I didn't want to admit that my inheritance was abhorrent—but it was that same losing, forgetting, refusing to look that condemned me all the same. When we insist on averting our gaze, it is our own sin to which we become most blind.

As theologian Esau McCaulley has observed, "Everybody's auntie was an abolitionist, but nobody owned slaves."

Then I read Ta-Nehisi Coates's essay "The Case for Reparations." I thought about the Vanderpool case file in the Special Collections Library and decided that fifty dollars for a set of copies just might be a gesture toward my own personal reparations. The donation I could make to the cause of decreasing ignorance—my own, if no one else's.

Or, I thought, I could spend the fifty dollars on gas and drive down to look at the documents myself.

So I bundled up my four children—then ages six, eight, ten, and twelve—and we barreled down the interstate through the broad, fertile Willamette Valley that had attracted so many of those early pioneers. The librarian had to yell at my two youngest children for attempting to ride a rolling chair down a hallway filled with artifacts and I had to send all four of them outside unattended to flip water bottles while I waited for the file to be pulled, but eventually I'd snapped a picture of every page of the Vanderpool file, rustled my kids up from where they'd moved on from water bottles to parkour, and plunked them down in the nearest Starbucks for a quick treat before we made our way north again.

"So, guys," I asked my children over Zombie Frappuccinos, "was it right that Oregon didn't allow Black people to live here?"

They pulled the straws out of their mouths long enough to yell "No!" in unison.

"And what should we do about it now?" I asked them.

But the straws had already been reinserted. Four sets of wide eyes stared at me while four pairs of busy cheeks worked the icy sugar.

I didn't know what the answer was either. My question hung in the air as we threw away our plastic cups and headed back out to the minivan.

And the years went by. Years in which I tried to find out more about Jacob Vanderpool, then stopped, then started again. Years in which I turned what little I'd learned about him into an essay and tried to find a place to publish it and failed. Years in which my children grew bigger, and sometimes we talked about racial injustice, but more often we didn't, and time unspooled in its quiet yet disquieting way. Then I hit upon the idea that I needed to look not just for Jacob Vanderpool but also for the White people around him. And after I delved into the life of Theophilus Magruder and uncovered his multigenerational legacy of tyranny and greed, I knew it was time to search again for my own inheritance. So I purchased a subscription to Ancestry.com. It took only ten minutes on that website to find what I'd long since mislaid.

Entering just the names and birthplaces of my four grandparents led to dozens of tabs labeled "Potential Father" and "Potential Mother," each preceding generation spiraling backward along every branch of my well-documented family tree, just waiting to be clicked and added to my own burgeoning file. Traveling back along my father's line, from one Williams to the next, I soon found Samuel Williams—born 1777 in Prince George's County, Maryland, and died 1859 in Lebanon, Kentucky. My great-great-great-great-great-grandfather. Clicking the button called "Hints," I discovered that another Ancestry user, presumably a distant cousin of my own, had attached a document to Samuel Williams's profile, titled simply "Estate." It was typed in a modern font, and no picture of the original was provided, but the words rang a distant bell. It was a transcription of the will my father had long ago sent me in the mail.

A statement given by the administrator of Samuel Williams, Sr.'s estate follows:

Slave	Alfred	$1007.00
"	Susan	$1100.00
"	Jim	$804.00
"	John	$727.00

I stared at the list for a long, long time. Names. They had *names*. The names of the human beings held as property by my ancestors were Alfred, Susan, Jim, and John.

I also found the 1850 Census Slave Schedule, which listed birth years and genders for enslaved members of the Samuel Williams household. The census showed that back in 1850, the household had also claimed four other enslaved members—an older man, a younger woman, and two young girls—so I couldn't know exactly how the names in the will matched up with the birth years in the census. Then I found a chart online showing average sale prices based on gender and age. By plotting the names and prices from the will against the birth years and genders in the census, I was able to deduce the ages of Alfred, Susan, Jim, and John. In 1859, when he was sold away from the Williams farm, Alfred was probably thirty-five. Jim and John, with their lower sale prices, were probably twelve and eleven. Susan, I guessed, was thirty-nine. I suspected that the other enslaved members of the household had been sold off, or died, in the years between the census and the will.

There was no way of knowing, but I imagined that perhaps Alfred, Susan, Jim, and John had been a nuclear family. Perhaps the two young girls from the 1850 census had belonged to them as well.

If Susan was thirty-nine when she was sold away from the Williams farm in 1859, then she would have been forty-three in 1863, when she was freed by the Emancipation Proclamation. The same age I was just then, as I was uncovering all of this.

I thought about all the phases of my life, all the things I'd done in my first forty-three years: grade school, high school, college, my years working as a teacher before my children were born, my years at home with young children, my years since returning to part-time work. By the time I was forty-three, I'd lived in seven states and traveled to sixteen countries. Aside from the fact that we'd both lived in Kentucky, Susan would have shared none of these core life experiences. I was stunned as I tried to comprehend the vast gulf between my own life and the life of the woman who had been enslaved by my ancestor.

Yet if I was right that Susan was the mother of all the children listed on the 1850 census, then she and I did share one powerful human experience. We each may have grown four babies in our wombs, nursed four babies at our breasts, carried four babies in our arms. The age span of Susan's children—if they were her children—was strikingly similar to my own. In 1859, hers were fifteen, fourteen, twelve, and eleven; as I uncovered all this, mine were sixteen, fourteen, twelve, and ten. The next week, my husband and I would be getting on a plane to make a college visit with our sixteen-year-old daughter. When Susan was my age, she probably had no idea where her teenage daughters were. My youngest son still wanted me to climb in bed with him every night and pray for God to take his fears away. When Susan was about my age, she had to say goodbye to her two youngest sons, so close to the ages of my own two youngest sons. She probably never saw them again.

All this heartache, and for what? To enrich *my* family.

. . .

There is a certain story I can tell about my family's financial footing. My husband is the pastor of a small neighborhood church. I
have cobbled together a series of not-exactly-lucrative part-time
jobs: teacher, home-healthcare worker, freelance writer. We live in
a dilapidated old house in a working-class suburb of Portland with
our four children and my brother, who has been disabled since
birth and receives a monthly pittance from the Social Security Administration. We've had our share of WIC and free-lunch years.
We haven't saved enough for retirement or our children's college
educations. Most of our monthly income goes to the mortgage and
the grocery store. I have frequently known the agony of running
out of money before running out of month. We go camping for our
summer vacations, and our tent is busted.

This is the kind of story many Americans like to tell about ourselves. Our politicians wax on about heroic single mothers and
factory-worker fathers and the sheer durability of their own bootstraps. I wonder if some of us rush to describe our poverty because
we don't want to associate ourselves with wealth. Because we
know that in our country, oftentimes, wealth stinks.

Because there is another story I can tell about myself. This is the
story I don't often divulge: that between the contributions of my
parents and grandparents, my private college education was entirely paid for. That my parents paid for my first master's degree,
and my mom sold her house to help pay for my second one. That
between us, my husband and I have five post-secondary degrees to
our names, all from private institutions, and we've never made a

1

2

single student-loan payment. (My in-laws, bless them, paid off my husband's student loans themselves, always refusing to let us take them over.) My husband's grandmother gifted him with stocks, which we sold to purchase our first car, and we've never taken out a car loan since. A previous church gave us a down-payment loan to buy our first house. When my children were born, my grandmother set them up with education trust funds: ten thousand dollars in stocks, each. At every turn, what we've needed has been handed to us.

The value of what I have received is astronomical. But how much of it came from interest compounded on slavery's ill-gotten gain?

There was the sale of Alfred, Susan, Jim, and John: a total of $3,638 dollars in 1859, or in 2023 currency, $131,130.18. And that was just their sale. While they lived with my family, Alfred, Susan, Jim, and John's labor was worth an average of $180,000 per person, in today's dollars, per year. For each year that he worked eight laborers, my five-times-great-grandfather would have stolen more than 1.4 million dollars' worth of labor from people who were never compensated. That's $1,440,000 *per year*. And that was just on one medium-sized farm in Kentucky.

He wasn't the only enslaver in my family either. Ancestry records revealed that Samuel was at least the third in a line of Williams men who'd passed their enslaved human property down to their descendants like so many feather mattresses.

And that was just one branch of my family tree. I found slavery on my mother's side too. I hadn't even realized that her ancestors hailed from the South. I knew about the Latourettes on my mother's mother's side, but all I'd ever known of my mother's father's family was that my maternal grandfather had been raised in Seattle. Two clicks of a button revealed that his father had been born in North Carolina. Directly along my Lucas family line was another series of slaveholders. These newly discovered wills recorded even more enslaved household members than the wills in my father's family. "One Negro man called Kary, one Negro woman called Beck, and one Negro woman called Pink . . . one Negro girl called Aggai . . . one Negro girl of equal value to the above mentioned Aggai . . . one Negro boy called Abram . . . one Negro boy called Arthur . . . one Negro boy"—all of them, wrote my ancestor Lewis Lucas in 1806, comprised "this worldly Estate wherewith it has pleased God to bless me."

All those lives. All that labor. All that profit. All of it, my ancestor supposed, a gift from God.

It isn't hard to trace the monetary effects of slavery in my family lines. The money that passed from father to son through generations of both the Williams and the Lucas lines enabled those men to become pharmacists, doctors, businessmen, bankers. Perhaps they endured seasons of penny-pinching. Perhaps they would argue, if they were here, that they pulled themselves up by those ubiquitous bootstraps. But the socioeconomic capital of millions of dollars' worth of slave labor must have been a powerful buoy. How much of it had come down to me? How could I even begin to measure it?

I know that many White Americans don't carry stories—or wallets—like these in their back pockets. I'm sure that grappling with our nation's history of slave-inflated wealth hits differently for White people who cannot see quite so clearly the ways slavery might have economically benefited their own families. The truth is that income inequality in the United States *has* pushed many White families, as well as families of color, into poverty. In this arena, I appreciate the work of groups like Showing Up for Racial Justice, which organizes White people from all socioeconomic backgrounds and focuses on the importance of acknowledging socioeconomic class in the fight for racial justice.

On the one hand, it's important to remember that racism was a wedge the wealthy used to divide the poor. Heather McGhee argues powerfully in *The Sum of Us* that the tactics employed to economically wound Black Americans ended up hurting everyone.

On the other hand, we cannot lose sight of the way every White American did gain, albeit sometimes indirectly, from the activities of the slaveholding few. "In the teaching of American history," wrote scholars Karen E. Fields and Barbara J. Fields, "perhaps the most difficult lesson to convey is that slavery once held the entire country in its grip. It was not just the business of enslaved black people, slaveholders, or the South. Slavery engaged an immense geography of connected activities that no Americans could escape, wherever they were and whenever they lived." America—what we like to call the richest nation on earth—was built on the backs of the enslaved.

I wanted to imagine that my ancestors were, at least, kind and gentle slave owners. Wouldn't that be nice? Maybe they were just caught in an economic machine they couldn't extract themselves from. Maybe Samuel treated Alfred, Susan, Jim, and John with generosity and dignity.

The myth of the kind enslaver has traveled far and wide in America. We soften our guilt this way, I suppose. Movies, romance novels, sermons, and school curricula all paint the fantasy of the benevolent slave owner. But this terrible, ironic fantasy must be repudiated. There can be no kindness or dignity in enslaving people, no matter how much porridge you give them for breakfast.

In any case, all evidence lay to the contrary. I found an oral history online, taken from a formerly enslaved man named Carl Boone. Boone was enslaved in Lebanon, Kentucky, the same small town where my ancestors had lived with the people they'd enslaved. Born "fifteen years before the close of the Civil War," he would have been about the same age as Jim and John. Boone recalled that "all the colored folk on plantations and farms around our plantation were slaves and most of them were terribly mistreated by their masters." In all likelihood, the treatment Alfred, Susan, Jim, and John received from Samuel Williams was as terrible as the rest.

Boone recalled one horrible incident with clarity:

> After committing a small wrong, Master Thompson became angry, tied his slave to a whipping post and beat him terribly. Mrs. Thompson begged him to quit whipping, saying, "You might kill him," and the master replied that he aimed to kill him. He then tied the slave behind a horse and dragged him over a fifty acre field until the slave was dead.

This is the world—the same small town, even—where my ancestors lived with their enslaved household. A world in which a White man's rage could not be checked and would be allowed to run rampant until it culminated in the most horrific forms of torture.

Imagine being enslaved in such a place. Imagine the mortal terror such a story would instill as it was whispered from plantation to plantation.

Imagine being White in such a place. Imagine the hardness with which you would have to encase your heart in order to continue worshipping and shopping and visiting with your neighbor Master Thompson. To believe his conduct ordinary and justifiable. To exercise some form of it yourself.

How much of the violence that erupts in our society today points to a multigenerational lineage of brutality running straight back to the days of Alfred, Susan, Jim, and John?

As I combed back through the records of my ancestors, looking for entries in the 1850 Census Slave Schedule or for wills that specifically mentioned the disbursement of human "property," I recognized a place name that seemed familiar: Prince George's County, Maryland. According to Ancestry records, Prince George's County was the 1777 birthplace of Samuel Williams, the man whose death in 1859 had prompted the sale of Alfred, Susan, Jim, and John. Prince George's County was also the place where Samuel's father, John Williams—who had fought in the Revolutionary War right around the time he sired Samuel—had lived his entire life. And Prince George's County was the place where John's father, Stockett Williams, had lived and died. Before moving out to Kentucky, three generations of my family's enslavers had lived in Prince George's County, Maryland.

As I went back to remind myself why that name sounded familiar, I found that Prince George's County, Maryland, was also the place where Theophilus Magruder's father, Patrick Henry Magruder, was born. Magruder's family and my own family had both lived in Prince George's County in the 1700s. That might mean nothing, I realized, but it might mean that they had been neighbors, or served on the same county commission, or attended the same church.

Then I found an entry in the book *Colonial Families of the USA, 1607–1775* that listed a Magruder and a Williams on the same page. Further comparison of Theophilus Magruder's family tree with my own led me to a common ancestor: one Thomas Sprigg, who came from England and died in Prince George's County in 1704. When the Williams family and the Magruder family lived in Prince George's County together throughout the 1700s, they were not simply neighbors or acquaintances; they were cousins. Ancestry helpfully informed me that Theophilus Magruder, whom I read as the clear villain in Jacob Vanderpool's story, was my own fourth cousin, seven times removed. I could turn up my nose at the horrors of Theophilus Magruder's behavior, but I could not ignore that he was one of my own.

And what of Prince George's County, the place where those particular branches of both my own and Theophilus Magruder's American stories began? It borders Washington, D.C. Its residents—like Patrick Henry Magruder, the congressman, Li-

brarian of Congress, and early federal embezzler—shaped our na-
scent country. Prince George's County was also home to the
highest proportion of enslaved residents of any county in Maryland.

What struck me as I uncovered all this was just how interconnected our American stories truly were. Samuel Williams died in
Lebanon, Kentucky, in the shadow of the looming Civil War, but
he was conceived in Maryland, in the midst of the American Revolution. Theophilus Magruder may have acquired his attitude toward African Americans on his parents' natal plantations on the
East Coast, but he took that prejudice across the country with him
to Oregon. I was used to thinking of history as a series of discrete
events: These people did this thing in this place at this time, while
those other people did that other thing in that other place at that
other time. As I looked for my own roots, I was reminded that
sometimes this thing and that thing were done by the very same
people. Or at least by people who were all related.

And by looking at the life spans of all these forebears, I remembered again just how long a human life can be. It was conceivable—
perhaps not likely, but possible—that John, the youngest enslaved
person sold from my great-great-great-great-great-grandfather's
farm, had lived to be ninety, dying in 1937. If he had, he might
have held in his arms, at the end of his life, a baby who could still
be alive today. All the distinct events that added up to the history
of America from slavery to now had taken place in just two long
lifetimes.

I realized, as well, that what is meant by "my family" gets awfully diffuse the further back we go. We all have two biological
parents, four grandparents, eight great-grandparents, and so on—

the number of our direct ancestors doubles with each preceding generation. By the time I get back to Thomas Sprigg, the ancestor I share with Theophilus Magruder, he's one of 4,096 biological tenth great-grandparents I can claim. The math in reverse is even more mind-boggling. According to one estimate I found, assuming only three descendants per couple (quite conservative considering the number of children those early colonial families used to have), by the time you get down to tenth great-grandchildren, each ancestor can be presumed to have almost 800,000 direct descendants. The International Society of Genetic Genealogy says that we each have more than one million tenth cousins.

We are all related, of course. From Adam and Eve, from Noah and his wife, from the very first *Homo sapiens* on down—take your pick of a starting place—we're all some number of cousin, some number of times removed, on the human family tree. This is a fact that's often used in discussions about race to argue for our shared humanity. And that's true and worth dwelling on. But in the nearer term of our shared American history, for White people in particular, we must acknowledge that *we* are all related. For those of us whose ancestors came from Europe to America sometime after 1607, whether we can pick our way up and down the Ancestry family trees to find one another or not, there's a pretty decent chance that somewhere along the way, one of the 800,000-plus descendants of one of my 4,096 tenth great-grandparents married one of the 800,000-plus descendants of one of your 4,096 tenth great-grandparents. In other words, the history of White people in America is *our* history.

I have to admit that, for much of my life, I didn't want to know this. I didn't want to acknowledge that the contorted faces of the White people screaming in protest at the integration of Southern schools belonged to *my people*. That the men under the white hoods were *my people*. That the masters holding the whips, the mobs tightening the lynching nooses, the policemen firing the fatal shots, the doctors conducting the experiments, the judges handing down the unjust sentences, the city planners drawing the red lines, and on and on and on, were *my people*. But of course they were. I did not spring whole from the ground on the day of my birth.

Who else's people would they be?

I do not know how to return what my ancestors stole. I do not know how to pay back what I owe to the descendants of the ones my ancestors stole from.

I sometimes imagine it is enough to be generous. To assuage my guilt by passing granola bars out the car window at stoplights or writing an occasional check to a nonprofit downtown. But the opposite of greed is not simply generosity. Generosity, in fact, can be toxic. The subtle toxicity of generosity is that it keeps me in the driver's seat. When I imagine I am giving away the leftovers of money that belongs to me, I retain control. But this is a myth, because wealth that has been stolen—even by my ancestors—does not rightfully belong to me.

This lesson hit home for me in a moment that still grieves me.

Only one African American man attended our church in Oregon. His name was Loy. Gradually, Loy and I became friends. We bonded over a shared love of books. We made plans to someday teach writing classes together in the Oregon State Penitentiary.

Over bagels and coffee, Loy told me of his struggles—that over the seven decades of his life, he had encountered every kind of racism imaginable. That he struggled to find employment. That he sometimes lived in his van. But it was clear to me as he talked that Loy's most important possession was his dignity. So rather than offer handouts, my husband and I occasionally employed him for odd jobs around the house. One winter, we gave Loy five hundred dollars as a deposit on some landscaping work that he planned to complete the following spring. It was not enough to get him out of his van, but it was all we could afford.

Then Loy died. Not long afterward, I pulled up to my house, full of grief over the loss of my friend, and my gaze drifted to my weedy lawn. I realized that Loy would never complete the work we had paid him for. *Oh well*, I thought, *maybe he's working right now on getting my heavenly home ready for me someday.*

And then the full horror of that thought struck me, and I sat there in shame. Had I really imported the warped power dynamics of our broken world into my concept of heaven? Did I imagine that even in the hereafter, my friend would owe me his lawn-care services? How horrifying. Yet this is where my mind had gone.

Loy's last name was William, but he had changed it from Williams. He and I were born with the same last name. There are lots of Williamses, both White and Black, in this country. But isn't it possible that my friend could have been descended from Alfred, Susan, Jim, and John? That my direct ancestors had stolen their millions of dollars' worth of slave labor from Loy's direct ancestors? And here I was, imagining that *he* was the one who owed something to *me*. That the same dynamics of server and served that had gripped our families for hundreds of years would continue into *eternity.*

I had never owned slaves or driven a business competitor away. Perhaps I wasn't as greedy as Theophilus Magruder or as tight-fisted as Samuel Williams. But I was so shaped by my membership in their family that I actually believed my measly generosity incurred a debt that would extend beyond the grave.

Father, forgive me.

The last shall be first, says Jesus, and the first shall be last. But we cannot wait for eternity to begin to repair the damage we and our people have inflicted. And it is not enough simply to imagine ourselves generous. The opposite of greed is prying our clenched fingers all the way open and recognizing that what sits in our palms does not belong to us at all. It never did.

Chapter Five

The Judge

Portrait of Thomas Nelson, circa 1857.
From *Portraits of Eminent Americans Now Living*.

P art of the reason I had driven to Eugene to see the Vanderpool case files was because I wanted to find an address.

It bothered me that I'd spent all my time searching for Jacob
Vanderpool online, when the physical location of his home and
workplace was just around the corner. "Main Street, opposite the
Statesman Office." But where on Main Street was the *Statesman*
office?

I thought that if I could just find out exactly where Vanderpool's building had stood, maybe I could walk to the spot and . . . well, I wasn't sure what I'd do there. Pay my respects? Apologize? Whisper my condolences into the ether?

But it didn't matter, because in the entire Jacob Vanderpool file, there was no address. Just a set of mimeographed papers with the values reversed: little white handwritten notes scratched into a field of black. And a set of typed transcripts that someone had marked up with pencil and blue highlighter. Three sets of documents in all: Theophilus Magruder's sworn affidavit. The warrant for Vanderpool's arrest. The records from the trial proceedings. No address. I could walk up and down Main Street from one end to the other—and I did, from the defunct paper mill at the west end to the boat-storage lot on the east side—but I had no way of knowing where, exactly, Jacob Vanderpool had begun to build his dreams, or where he might have stood and grieved as it all came crashing down.

Then I was called to jury duty.

The county courthouse is a classic 1936 building that stands in the middle of Oregon City's Main Street. Our day began in the annex building next door, with a video on implicit bias. Judges of various races pleaded with us to "be aware and be fair." Eventually, thirteen potential jurors were chosen, and we wound our way over to the main building, where they told us to sit and wait in an empty upstairs courtroom.

I pulled a book out of my bag, *Unsettling Truths: The Ongoing, Dehumanizing Legacy of the Doctrine of Discovery,* by Mark Charles and Soong-Chan Rah. As I sat there in the windowless marble-floored courtroom, waiting for my turn to be an instrument of whatever justice this system had to offer, I read about Charles's Navajo practice of waking each morning to watch the sun rise and bless the Creator. The contrast between the two cultures struck me; my eyes filled with tears.

Then the case was dismissed. Truth be told, I was disappointed. I wanted to serve, to be some force for justice. Years before, I'd played the role of Juror 8 in a high school production of *12 Angry Men*. Juror 8 is the one who saves the day, convincing the other jurors to reconsider the damning evidence and thereby uncovering the truth of the defendant's innocence. But I would not be replaying my role as the lead in the high school play that day. I followed the other jurors out of the courtroom and down the stairs.

Earlier that morning, we'd filed from the annex building into the courthouse through a back door. We left, now, via the front hall. As I walked toward the front doors, I noticed a series of prints and photographs hanging on the wall, depicting the evolution of the Clackamas County courthouse over the years. Because I was walking out, not in, I progressed backward through time. Past the culmination of the exhibit, showing the present state of the courthouse with its overcrowding issues and electrical problems: a plea for voters to approve an upcoming bond for a brand-new space. Past a picture of the current courthouse as it had appeared in 1936, brick and mortar gleaming. Past the 1880s building that had stood here before that, complete with a cyclist on an old-fashioned big-wheeled bicycle. *Could there be . . .* I wondered as I made my way toward the front doors. *Could there be an image of the courthouse where they tried Jacob Vanderpool?*

And then, just beside the metal detectors at the building's entrance, I saw a print of an old drawing. Beneath the sketch, a caption read, "Oregon City became the Territorial Capital and County Seat in 1843, and soon became a center of social and political life. This structure was erected 1849 to serve as the Capitol Building."

Erected 1849. This was it. The building where Jacob Vanderpool's trial had occurred. He'd probably been held as a prisoner in the building shown here for the four nights between his arrest on August 21 and his court appearance on August 25. *This* building, a precursor to the very building where I was now standing. Wherever else Jacob Vanderpool may have walked on Oregon City's Main Street, he had surely been *here.*

It was just a sketch. A wooden three-story structure with simple rows of windows and two small chimneys. Still, I felt I could almost see Jacob Vanderpool peering out from one of the windows. I stood there in the hallway, crowds of people thronging past me in both directions, and I stared into the blank windows of the drawing. What expression would I see on Vanderpool's face, I wondered, if I could see him looking back at me? Wistful? Resigned? Determined? Hopeful? Angry? Lonely? Desperate? Scared? If I could have stood on the sidewalk outside this building all those years ago and looked up into those eyes, what could I have said? What would I have done? I stared into the hand-drawn windows and felt myself tumbling 170 years back through time.

Suddenly I remembered where I was and glanced sheepishly

around the busy hallway. It was time for me to move on. But I knew I couldn't just keep walking. I asked the security guards operating the metal detector if I could take a picture.

"No," one replied. "No photographs in the courthouse."

"Could I just write down what this caption says?" I asked, and she nodded.

But I couldn't find a pen. I dug frantically through my purse—no pen anywhere. I apologized to the guards for my delay. One of them handed me a pen. I scribbled down the caption and made a hasty attempt to sketch Jacob Vanderpool's courthouse into my notebook.

The four guards all appeared to be people of color, Black and Latino. Everyone else I'd seen in the courthouse that day—the judges, the lawyers, the jury handlers, even most of the jury candidates—had appeared to be White. In the 170 years since Jacob Vanderpool had been expelled from the Oregon Territory in this same courthouse, people of color had made it back inside the front door, but not much farther.

When Jacob Vanderpool sat at trial in the wooden three-story courthouse on August 25, 1851, his case was not dismissed.

But an earlier case had been.

On a summer day in 1851, perhaps six weeks before *Theophilus Magruder v. Jacob Vanderpool*, some women from the Clackamas Tribe had gone out picking berries. Their ancestors had been picking berries on this same land for more than ten thousand years. But on this day, the women attracted the attention of a couple of White men who'd recently moved into the neighborhood.

The men were from the Johnson family—the patriarch of the clan, William Johnson, and his twenty-five-year-old son, Ezra. The Johnsons were the first permanent White settlers within the bounds of what is now the city of Portland. William Johnson had been elected High Sheriff of the original group of overland settlers and had participated in the first provisional government in 1843. After settling on the west side of the Willamette River and then moving east, the Johnsons finally ended up in an area that the Donation Land Claim map notes as, "Soil good. . . . Timber fir maple & Alder. Land rolling." The family farmed the land and operated a still, producing an alcohol known locally as "blue ruin." They also built a sawmill along what would come to be known as Johnson Creek. Today, their namesake creek runs along part of the boundary between the city of Portland and neighboring Clackamas County. I frequently enter and exit the freeway at Johnson Creek; sometimes I shop at the big-box stores in the shopping center known as Johnson Creek Crossing.

The only problem with the Johnson Creek area, for the Johnsons, was that it was still occupied by the Clackamas Tribe. In 1844, a visiting missionary to Oregon had remarked that the Indians were "rapidly wasting away, and the time is not far distant when the last deathwail will proclaim their universal extermination." But the White settlers could not wait for that last anticipated deathwail (which, it must be said, never came) before grabbing the land right out from under them. So, less than six months after passing the Donation Land Claim Act, which promised 320 acres to every White male or "half breed Indian" who wanted to settle in Oregon, in February 1851, Congress passed another law: the Indian Appropriations Act. With this law, the U.S. government gave itself permission to create a widespread reservation system, removing the land's Indigenous inhabitants to make space for the new settlers who had just been promised ownership. Anson Dart, the federally appointed superintendent of Indian affairs for the Oregon Territory, spent most of the year 1851 traveling throughout Oregon, establishing treaties and local reservations for some nineteen different tribes. Dart had approached the Clackamas people early in the year, but they had declined to sign. He'd moved on, with plans to return later.

And so, on that summer day in 1851, when the Clackamas women met the Johnson men out among the berries, a highly charged political miasma surrounded them. Perhaps the Johnsons knew that the Clackamas had refused to sign the treaty and wanted to intimidate them. Perhaps the women knew that their tribe had not yet signed, and wanted to take a stand. We don't know whether the Johnsons told them to leave or the women refused to go. All we know is that in the end, the Johnson men assaulted the Clackamas women, beating them violently.

When Dart, the Indian superintendent, heard about the attacks, he was distressed. The Clackamas treaty, which he had so far failed to negotiate, was the most important one to obtain because of the Clackamas people's proximity to Oregon City. By this time, the Clackamas Tribe had been greatly diminished by waves of European diseases. (Dart believed that the Clackamas were dying because they refused to eat bread made from wheat flour and insisted on eating salmon.) Still, despite the tribe's small numbers, conflict between the Clackamas Tribe and the Oregon City settlers could have been disastrous. When the Johnson attack occurred, Dart might have feared that the Clackamas Tribe would retaliate if he could not bring the men to justice or that they would be less trusting of his planned negotiations. So Dart convinced the Oregon Territory Supreme Court Justice to swear out a warrant for the men's arrest.

The Johnsons were brought to the wooden three-story courthouse. Leaders of the Clackamas Tribe, both men and women, thronged into the room. The trial began.

It was not the first time Indigenous people had seen the inside of the courthouse that stood on the site of their ancient fishing village. Previously, however, Indians had been the defendants, not on the side of the prosecution. The year before, five members of the Cayuse Tribe had stood trial in Oregon City for defending their land by killing thirteen members of the Whitman Mission in present-day Walla Walla, Washington. On June 3, 1850, a crowd had gathered in Oregon City to watch all five Cayuse men hang. They were later buried outside the city in unmarked graves.

In the Johnson case, Dart called as the first witness one of the Clackamas women who had suffered in the attack, a woman named Kezika. But when Kezika began to tell the story of how the Johnsons had beaten her, an objection was raised. Indian testimony was legally inadmissible. The Cayuse had not been permitted to testify on their own behalf in their trial the previous year either. Kezika's experience could be relayed to the court only if it had been witnessed by a White person. But no one except for the Johnson men and the Clackamas women had been present that day among the berries.

I first encountered this story when I found it in a handwritten letter that had been scanned and uploaded to the Yale University Library website. As I peered at the spidery, faded, sepia-toned handwriting on my computer screen, the scene sprang before my eyes: the plight of the women, whom the letter writer described as "squaws"; the callous disregard of the White men; the courtroom packed with Clackamas onlookers; the blatant White supremacy of the objector—and of the law on which the objection was based. I leaned forward in my chair, eager to find out what had happened in that hot July courtroom so many years ago.

"The objection was sustained," the letter continued. And that was that. Because there were no other witnesses to be had, the case was dismissed. An outcry rose up among the Clackamas people in the crowded courtroom. "Old Mr. Johnson" began to shout. The women produced "a volley of" something I could not decipher in the scribbled handwriting. Hilling? Ailing? Trilling? The Clackamas chiefs delivered "short but excited speeches." Somehow, amid the cacophony, the party dispersed, leaving the courtroom empty once again.

I was stunned. Who was writing this letter? It had to be someone who had been in the room that day. I scrolled to the end and found it signed by one Thomas Nelson.

I looked up from my computer screen and stared out the window, trying to remember. Thomas Nelson . . . it sounded familiar. Who was Thomas Nelson? Suddenly it hit me. Thomas Nelson was the same judge who would hear the Jacob Vanderpool case the following month. He'd been the judge in this trial as well.

Nelson had described the case in a letter he was writing home to his wife, who'd stayed behind in Upstate New York. ("With a little more regard for punctuation," Nelson admonished his wife in his opening paragraph, in critique of the letter he'd apparently just received from her, "and a little more observance of the rule which requires that the first letter of the word which begins a sentence should be a capital one, your proficiency in letter writing would be unquestioned.") After working as a lawyer in New York, Nelson had been appointed to the Oregon Territory Supreme Court just a few months before by President Millard Fillmore.

And just a few months before that, President Fillmore had presided over what would become his most notorious accomplishment: the passage of the Fugitive Slave Act. Under that law, a Black person suspected of having fled enslavement could be apprehended in any part of the United States and returned to the South without trial.

After he ended his first term, Fillmore shifted his political allegiance to the Know Nothing party, an anti-immigration, anti-Catholic nativist party that grew out of a "pureblood . . . Protestant Anglo-Saxon" secret society whose members were supposed to reply "I know nothing" when pressed.

Such were the political associations of Thomas Nelson, chief justice of the Oregon Territory Supreme Court—the man who believed he was merely upholding the law when he silenced the

Clackamas assault victims in July and expelled Jacob Vanderpool from Oregon in August.

The next time I read the sepia-toned letter (which had not, so far as I could tell, been transcribed anywhere), I did not skip to the end. I peered at the handwriting on my computer screen, forming the words aloud to make sure I was making sense of them, bumping along through all eight of its pages. And what I found in the paragraph below the account of the assault on the Clackamas women stunned me even more: "Our hotel has lately changed proprietors," Thomas Nelson wrote on July 21, 1851, "and its present management is a great improvement upon the old one."

Our hotel has lately changed proprietors. Thomas Nelson had arrived in Oregon City on the last day of April 1851 and had presumably been staying in a boarding house for the two and a half months since. Just thirteen days before Nelson wrote his letter, on July 8, 1851, Theophilus Magruder had taken out his ad in the paper, informing Oregon City that he had leased the Main Street Hotel and was undertaking a series of thorough repairs. Could the change of hotel proprietors in Judge Nelson's letter and Theophilus Magruder's new lease be one and the same? I turned to one of my new favorite JSTOR articles, a 1942 essay in the *Oregon Historical Quarterly* called "Survey of First Half-Century of Oregon Hotels." There was no record of any other hotels changing proprietors in Oregon City in July of 1851.* It had to be the same hotel. Judge Thomas

---

*Jacob Vanderpool himself, of course, had also recently begun operating a hotel, but he seems to have opened a new establishment rather than assumed proprietorship from a

Nelson must have been living in the hotel run by Theophilus Magruder when he heard the case Magruder brought against Jacob Vanderpool.

And its present management is a great improvement upon the old one. When Jacob Vanderpool faced that courtroom on August 25, 1851, less than a month after Nelson wrote those words, he faced not only a plaintiff who just happened to have a clear business interest in removing him from the Oregon Territory but also a judge who just happened to be enjoying the kind, domestic attentions of said plaintiff. Talk about a conflict of interest.

Judge Nelson enumerated in his letter all the things the new hotel proprietor had done for him. "They have given me a very snug bedroom," he wrote, "which is connected with a large and agreeable sitting room." One wonders whether Theophilus Magruder got the idea to put the chief justice of the Oregon Territory Supreme Court in the snug bedroom with its adjoining large and agreeable sitting room *before* or *after* he decided to haul his competitor to court. "Better than all," Nelson continued, "we rejoice weekly in clean sheets for our beds." He went on to explain that there was plenty of food but that it wasn't prepared quite as expertly as the food back home in New York. Apparently, whoever was in charge of Theophilus Magruder's kitchen hadn't yet learned that broiling beefsteak was, in Nelson's view, a superior method to frying it.

Thomas Nelson signed Theophilus Magruder's affidavit on a Wednesday. Jacob Vanderpool was brought into custody on a

---

previous owner. Furthermore, there is no indication that Vanderpool's Oregon Saloon and Boarding House would have been open in April, when Nelson arrived.

Thursday. Then they left him there all that long weekend to await trial. As Jacob Vanderpool might have tossed and turned in the jail just down the street, Thomas Nelson slumbered between clean sheets in a snug bedroom. He spent his private moments in a large and agreeable sitting room. He took his meals at Theophilus Magruder's plentiful table. Finally, on Monday morning, Thomas Nelson, chief justice of the Oregon Territory Supreme Court, walked to the wooden courthouse to begin hearing the case his own landlord was bringing against his business competitor.

When Dart returned to the Clackamas Tribe in November 1851—four months after the Johnson trial and three months after Vanderpool's—they did not again object to the terms of his treaty. Perhaps the Johnson trial had shown them that their resistance would go unheard. Dart promised the Clackamas people a local reservation, just as he had promised to each of the other eighteen tribes in Oregon, and a yearly annuity consisting of five hundred dollars in cash and two thousand dollars' worth of basic supplies like "twenty woolen coats . . . two barrels molasses . . . ten eight-quart tin kettles." But when Dart returned to Washington, D.C., with his nineteen treaties in hand, he found that he was too late. Pieces of the local reservations he'd planned to create had already been distributed to White settlers. Congress decided that it would be too expensive to buy out the pioneers, so they declined to ratify the treaties. The local reservations were never established. The government eventually consolidated multiple Oregon tribes into a smaller number of reservations in more remote, less desirable locations. The yearly annuities were never paid.

After I read the account of the Johnson-Clackamas case, I began to search the Oregon Donation Land Claim maps for the location of the Johnson settlement. I wanted to be sure that the Johnson Creek Johnsons were the only Johnsons "but a few miles from this place," as Nelson had written of his courtroom defendants. And I wanted to find the valuable land that had set off the violent attack on Kezika and her companions.

The Donation Land Claim maps are detailed and hand-drawn, the product of decades of surveys taken systematically in rectangular sections all across Oregon. They contain notes about the quality of the soil, topographical features like mountains and rivers, early roads, and the precise location of each land claim made under the Donation Land Claim Act, with the surname of the homesteader who laid claim to it. The areas closest to Oregon City were done first, with the surveyors spreading out from there as settlers gobbled up more and more of the territory.

But the website that hosted the maps was complex, with little instruction for the lay user. Each of the hundreds of maps was contained in a zip file that had to be downloaded before it could be opened. They were labeled according to a system the early pioneers had devised, based on imaginary lines called the Willamette Baseline and the Willamette Meridian. I peered at the tiny key, which for some reason I could not zoom in on, and tried to guess whether map 02s03e or 04n01w would provide the location I was looking for. It took a few downloads before I hit upon Oregon City. I branched out from there. After drawing myself a key on a sheet of scratch paper to keep track of which maps I'd already downloaded, I carefully opened maps to the east, west, south, and north, scanning each one for the word *Johnson*.

Unexpectedly, when I opened the map just south of Oregon City, I saw my ancestor's name. L. D. C. Latourette. I'd seen the Victorian houses labeled "Latourette" downtown and the park named after one of my cousins, but somehow seeing the name on this 1854 map made it more real. They were really here. All this time. All the way back then. My own family members had been in that first generation of Oregonians, the ones who'd stolen the land right out from under the Clackamas people, even as they'd waited in vain for the tribe's "last deathwail."

As I studied the map of Oregon City itself, my eyes sweeping left and right, looking for those Johnsons, I stopped when I saw what was closest to my own house.

I lived just a few blocks from the Clackamas River, a smaller tributary that flows into the Willamette just below the falls. We walked our dogs to the river almost every day. In the summer, the natural pool down the street from our house became our favorite swimming hole. We walked out the front door in our swimsuits and jumped off the rocks into the glacier-fed stream several times a week. And right there, on the bank of the Clackamas River just down from the house I was then sitting in, some mid-nineteenth-century surveyor had carefully drawn several little triangles marked "Indian Village" and several little tombstones marked "Indian Graves."

I had always known, of course, in the abstract way that anyone who owns a piece of North America knows, that the land I currently hold title to had once been occupied by someone else. But seeing those little tombstones took my breath away. I somehow hadn't allowed myself to consider that they had all been here together. That in the same year Jacob Vanderpool was held in the courthouse downtown, my great-great-great-great-uncle Latourette was already living on his land claim on the hill, and the Clackamas Indians were still burying their dead in the place where I would someday walk with my children to go swimming.

It wasn't the way I had always preferred to imagine—that the American Indians, with their beautiful civilization, had slunk quietly away after the first European contact and that several centuries later, somebody in my family had rolled in to an empty prairie and picked out an auspicious spot to set up shop. No. They were all here at the same time, jostling for position in this land of mild, rainy Januarys and glorious blue-sky Julys. The question of who would dominate these rivers, trees, soil, and rocks had never actually been much of a question. They would belong—because of the weapons they wielded in their hands and in their immune systems—to the people who believed, based on an arbitrary hierarchy of melanin, that they were the only human beings with any rights at all.

The night after I found the Indian tombstones marked on the Donation Land Claim map, I walked down to the riverbank with my dogs.

As my feet slapped the asphalt, I wondered if the land's original inhabitants would even recognize this place now. The land itself has been smoothed and leveled, each lawn as flat as the floorboards that sit on it. It has also been gridded into a series of parallel and perpendicular lines: streets meet driveways meet sidewalks meet curbs meet streets, all neatly delineated by yellow paint, fencing, and edged grass. It is all just as Thomas Jefferson had envisioned when he aspired to divide the United States of America into "an almost infinite number of squares."

Willie James Jennings remarked on Jefferson's plan, "The grid pattern of sellable squares of land signified the full realization of property ownership. It also displayed the complete remaking of indigenous land." Just as the little squares on the Donation Land Claim maps represented the incursion of settlers onto Indigenous land, the right angles on my street demonstrated a way of thinking about land and property that would have been utterly foreign to the land's first occupants.

But some of the land's original features remain. Some of the trees still grow. Not many of the old ones, since the White settlers clear-cut most of them in the nineteenth century. But a few towering cedars stretch from chain link to chain link, tall enough that they might at least have been saplings back when the Clackamas rested in their shade. Peering into the branches filling my neighbor's backyard, I wondered if Kezika and her companions might have reached out to steady themselves by that very trunk as they returned to their village after the attack at Johnson Creek.

And the rocks—certainly, the rocks were here. The land has been scaped within yards of the river, but at the last second, it tumbles down to meet the water in a joyful rush of unreconstructed rock. As I approached the rock formations, my feet instinctively slowed. My dogs tugged at their leashes while I studied the rugged remnants of some ancient and faraway volcano. These rocks form the seats where I perch in the summer to watch my children dive for crawdads. They become heating pads that hold the sun's warmth for me until I'm hot enough to jump in myself. They greet me, still warm, when I drag myself, shivering, out of the water again. These rocks have surely been here this whole time.

For ten thousand years, generation after generation after generation after generation of Clackamas men and women and boys and girls must have sat on these very same rocks, warming their toes on these very same ledges. These rocks formed the edge of their final village, where they were banished after the White settlers started to take over the spot at the falls of the Willamette, a couple of miles away. And as their time in this land was ending— not long before the order came to march seventy miles west to the Grand Ronde Reservation—some Clackamas mother with her children might have stood, just for a moment, where I was standing now. Maybe she looked across the river and saw Lyman D. C. Latourette, or even Jacob Vanderpool, standing on the other side.

I could almost see them now. The mother and child in their leather tunics on this side of the river. The two men in buttoned shirts and trousers on the other, one with skin just a disqualifying shade darker than the other. American Indian, Black, White—in 1851, they had all been here, all at the same time. All could have stayed—together—if not for my own ancestors' determination to drive everyone else away.

My eyes drifted down to the river—another land feature that had been here all this time. This river, the Clackamas, bubbled into existence high in the mountains eighty miles away. It charged down to the flatlands, where it fed into the Willamette, which fed into the Columbia, which fed into the sea. The rivers resisted right angles and straight lines. They might be controlled, but they could not be contained.

Occasionally, I had seen American Indians holding drum circles on the patch of grass between the water and the road. I had never realized that it was because this was a burial site—never realized the magnitude of what they might be memorializing here. But that night, there was only a group of amorous teenagers clambering over the rocks. Some jumped into the water, some groped one another, and some yelled loudly.

I missed the sound of those drums, so I pulled up powwow chants on my headphones. Later, I switched over to the Apsáalooke hip-hop artist Supaman. As the rhythmic pulse of Supaman's "Prayer Loop Song" filled my ears, I walked out onto the rocks that edged the river and tried to imagine the modern world away. I tried to block out the freeway, and the old concrete pylons, and the houses on the opposite bank. I tried to imagine the riverbanks filled with trees instead of office buildings. I couldn't quite see it, so I concentrated instead on the rocks: those ancient stepping stones that had surely looked the same back when the Clackamas people had gathered here. Back before Chief Justice Thomas Nelson had decreed that in this land, the voices of both Indigenous and Black people would be silenced.

I hopped down to the water, jumping from one rock to the next. I ran my hands through the dry grasses that here and there found purchase in the crevices. I popped a couple of wild blackberries into my mouth, and no one assaulted me.

Chapter Six

From Supremacy to Shalom

How inextricably interwoven the past is in the present, how heavily that past bears on the future; we cannot talk about black lives mattering or police brutality without reckoning with the very foundation of this country.

　　—Jesmyn Ward, *The Fire This Time*

When I kept silent,
　　my bones wasted away
　　through my groaning all day long.

　　—Psalm 32:3

During the last week of August 1851, while Jacob Vanderpool sweated out the wait for his trial, White supremacy in America was running hot. The previous twelve months had seen the passage of both the Fugitive Slave Act *and* the Indian Appropriations Act. All over the continent, White people were busy establishing themselves as the ultimate arbiters of everyone else's fate. And as Vanderpool would discover, the fever dream of White dominion over Black bodies and Indigenous lands had already reached the Oregon Territory Supreme Court. In July, Chief Justice Thomas Nelson had thrown Kezika's case out of his courtroom; soon, he would throw Vanderpool out of Oregon.

In truth, White America's treatment of the people they found on this continent and the people they imported from another one has always been a one-two punch. The psychological groundwork White colonizers needed to internalize in order to force Africans into race-based chattel slavery was laid by their racialization and attempted genocide of North America's Indigenous inhabitants. As the colonists, and those who came after them, trained themselves to view American Indians as "other," it paved the way for seeing Black Americans as "other" too.

"In order to exploit others for your own gain," wrote Heather McGhee, "you have to first sever the tie between yourself and them." The tie that bound Europeans to the rest of the world had been severed as far back as 1452, when Pope Nicholas V issued the first papal bull of the Doctrine of Discovery. The pope granted Christian monarchs religious permission

> to invade, search out, capture, vanquish, and subdue all Saracens and pagans whatsoever, and other enemies of Christ wheresoever placed, and the kingdoms, dukedoms, principalities, dominions, possessions, and all movable and immovable goods whatsoever held and possessed by them and to reduce their persons to perpetual slavery and to apply and appropriate to himself and his successors the kingdoms, dukedoms, counties, principalities, dominions, possessions, and goods, and to convert them to his and their use and profit.

Perpetual slavery for all who were not like them; all their goods and labor stolen for European profit. This was the sanctioned order from the head of the entire Western Christian church. Mark Charles and Soong-Chan Rah wrote in *Unsettling Truths: The Ongoing, Dehumanizing Legacy of the Doctrine of Discovery* about how the implications of that doctrine still reverberate in the New World, more than half a millennium later.

In the fifteenth century, the concept that all the world's diverse peoples might fit into a handful of "races" had not yet been invented. Pope Nicholas V had to explain whom he meant to subserviate with words like *Saracens, pagans,* and *enemies of Christ.* But by the mid-nineteenth century, the concept of race and the supremacy of the White one were treated as well-established facts. When the objection to Kezika's testimony was raised, simply because she was not White, Chief Justice Nelson wasted no time in sustaining it. Jacob Vanderpool would meet a similar fate. When Oregon's settlers wanted Indigenous land or when Southern plantation owners wanted Black labor, it was clear to all of them, based on the myth of White supremacy that had been propped up by scientists and theologians alike for four hundred years, that there was absolutely no reason for them not to take it.

As I followed Jacob Vanderpool's story all the way back to the first European footsteps on this continent and then all the way forward to me, I noticed that when I started talking about my ancestors' sins, some people got nervous.

"America is a good place," a friend of mine insisted, her voice shaking with emotion. "I know it in my bones." From the Pilgrims to the pioneers, my friend was proud of her White ancestors. She was deeply hesitant to talk about racism, past or present, lest we somehow unseat all the goodness she knew was here.

My friend was not alone. In September 2020, the Trump White House put out a statement condemning "blame-focused diversity training" and calling the idea that our country is fundamentally racist "a lie." According to the statement, the concept that "an individual, by virtue of his or her race or sex, bears responsibility for actions committed in the past by other members of the same race or sex" was "divisive"; therefore, such discussion was banned from all federal workplaces. In the years since, a kind of moral panic has emerged around some parents' fears that if their children learn the truth about our country's history of slavery or segregation, they will be harmed. As of February 2022, "at least 36 states have adopted or introduced laws or policies that restrict teaching about race and racism."

Other Americans, of course, know in their bones that America's fundamental racism not only exists but also causes physical, psychological, economic, and spiritual harm every single day. From the very first European explorers' disregard of the land's Indigenous inhabitants, to the Constitution's reckoning of each African American as three-fifths of a person, to slavery, to Jim Crow, to segregation, to redlining, to lynching, to the school-to-prison pipeline, to unemployment rates, to wage gaps, to knees on necks and disproportionate numbers of deaths from coronavirus—for Americans of color, there is no escape from the architecture of White supremacy. "Where can I go," a Black friend of mine recently lamented, "where people don't hate me?"

It is our inability to reconcile these two narratives—the good Pilgrims whose faults we dare not face; the reality of hundreds of years of White supremacy we cannot ignore—that even now threatens to fracture our society. "The heart of our nation's problem with race," said Mark Charles, "is that we do not have a common memory." If we cannot agree on what has already happened, we will never agree on how to move forward. And if White Americans do not take responsibility for actions committed in the past by members of our race, who will?

As I tried to confront the actions of my ancestors, I found myself turning again and again to my Bible. In its pages, I found example after example of places where ancestors' value was not discounted even as their sins were fully explored. The same Bible that told me to honor my father and mother, the same Bible that set up its patriarchs and matriarchs as examples of the faith—this same Bible, I saw, held its ancestors unswervingly to the light of truth.

Who could imagine that the foreign slave Hagar, "victimized" by the patriarch of the faith and "abused" by its matriarch, would be given space in the pages of her enslavers' Bible to tell her own story? Who could imagine that David the king would be revealed as David the adulterer? That Paul the apostle would be Saul the murderer? That Jacob would be a liar, Judah a hypocrite, Peter a betrayer, Noah a drunk? The Bible pulled skeleton after skeleton out of closet after closet, until at last it dawned on me that maybe honoring those who came before me had to begin with being honest about them.

The Bible characters themselves were honest about their own

ancestors' sins. At times, they even went so far as to *repent* of their ancestors' sins, as when Daniel prayed, "We and our kings, our princes and our ancestors are covered with shame, LORD, because we have sinned against you." *Repent* is a loaded word that conjures up darkened confessional booths and hair shirts, but the Greek word *metanoia* simply means to change one's mind—or, as my pastor husband explains, to "think bigger, think differently, or think again." When the people of the Bible repented of their ancestors' sins, they were thinking again, with a bigger perspective, about what their ancestors did—allowing God's truth to recast their ancestors' actions in a new light. True repentance leads to new action, but it begins with new thought.

I found myself drawn to the book of Nehemiah, where the people of God had returned to Israel after seventy years of exile in Babylon. With a festival unlike any other in their nation's history, the people wept, ate, rejoiced, and finally "stood in their places and confessed their sins and the sins of their ancestors."

What would it look like, I wondered, for America to do something similar? For our nation to set apart, as Claudia Rankine called for, "a sustained state of national mourning for black lives"? Simply to allow ourselves to *think again*, together, about our past? To acknowledge our ancestors' wrongs by thinking about them with a bigger perspective? To think differently about whose testimony is worth hearing, whose lands worth defending, whose bodies worth protecting?

Other countries have already undertaken the work of corporate repentance. In 2010, the government of Cameroon funded a visit to that nation for American descendants of enslaved Cameroonians, where tribal chiefs delivered an official apology for their ancestors' role in selling their own people into slavery. Other African countries have done similar work. Germany holds an annual Holocaust remembrance ceremony, makes Holocaust awareness an "integral part of public school education," and has given more than ninety billion dollars to Holocaust survivors. In 1992, the president of South Africa publicly apologized for apartheid, and its government went on to pay eighty-five million dollars to victims of apartheid crimes.

In the United States of America, by contrast, no reparations for descendants of enslaved African Americans have ever been paid. In fact, the United States paid reparations to its *enslavers*. The District of Columbia Compensated Emancipation Act set aside one million dollars to compensate slaveholders for the loss of their "property." But reparations are not just about money. Ereshnee Naidu-Silverman wrote that reparations can be meaningful "only if accompanied by a public truth-telling project that addresses continued white denialism, exposes the reality of racism and makes clear the consequences of decades of inaction."

This kind of corporate repentance has its potential pitfalls, as C. S. Lewis pointed out in his 1940 essay "Dangers of National Repentance." Writing in the context of young British Christians grieved about their country's involvement in World War II, Lewis worried that national repentance was merely a smoke screen for "turn[ing] from the bitter task of repenting our own sins to the congenial one of bewailing—but, first, of denouncing—the conduct of others." Lewis was right: If by "national repentance" we mean "publicly announcing the ways in which our political enemies have failed," we will certainly end up in a worse spiritual place than we started. It's critical that the Israelites in the book of

Nehemiah confessed *their* sins, as well as their ancestors'. Reflecting on Lewis's essay in 2017, Marvin Hinten wrote, "If people use the word 'we' in confessional prayer, whether in church or anywhere else, at least some of the sins confessed should be their own."

To put a finer point on it: If I wanted to imagine some future moment when all of America would gather to repent of its White supremacist past, I needed to begin by examining the White supremacy in my own heart.

Not long after I began researching Jacob Vanderpool, I ran into a couple of old friends at a high school football game. Five years earlier, we'd attended the same church, back when we'd lived in the same city. Our families had run in the same circles—the same Sunday night potlucks and men's fellowship groups and women's Bible studies—but we weren't close enough that we'd stayed in touch. So I didn't know what was coming when I squeezed into the bleachers next to Cindy and asked, "How's church?"

Her eyes cut to her husband, Jon. "We . . . left," Cindy stammered.

"Oh." I tried to keep my voice even. My husband had been a pastor at that church before we'd left town, and I didn't want them to think I would take their departure personally. "Was it . . . just . . ." I trailed off, failing to supply a reason.

"Honestly, it got too political," Jon said, and Cindy nodded beside him. "Pastor Dave, he—he started talking about racism all the time."

Cindy's thin red hair danced in the breeze. Jon's pale-green eyes stared earnestly back at mine from behind his horn-rimmed glasses. I said nothing.

"Seriously, Sarah," he continued, "you wouldn't believe some of the things he was saying. He said that he's racist! That all White people are racist! You know how many retired missionaries to Africa there are at that church. Can you believe Dave said that to *them*?"

A shout went up in the stands around us, and we all glanced down at the football field, where one team had just scored a touchdown. Almost all the players on both teams were White. Almost everyone in the stands was White. Jon, Cindy, and I were White. The Black population in the Oregon town where we were sitting was 1.07 percent.

There was something ironic about White people debating whether White people are racist while nestled in the bleachers of a system that had somehow managed to keep everybody but White people out of the football stadium that night. But I did not speak to my friends about systemic racism or the history of Oregon's exclusion laws. I did not ask them why the very mention of the word *racism* had sent them running from a long-cherished community. Instead, as the noise of the crowd momentarily made continued conversation impossible, I bit my tongue and thought back to my own missionary days. It was on a short-term mission trip to Africa that I had first caught the stench of my own racism.

I first realized White supremacy lived in me on my first morning in Malawi. At twenty years old, I had traveled halfway around the world for a six-month internship in international development. All my life I'd seen pictures of African children sitting in the dust, all distended bellies and sad eyes, and I couldn't wait to cradle them in my arms. I wanted to spend myself on behalf of the needy, but I was about to discover the depth of my own neediness.

I woke up, in the house where I was staying with a relief worker from Uganda, after a disorienting sleep that followed the two back-to-back overnight flights, from Seattle to London and London to Lilongwe. I got out of bed and shuffled to the window to look down into the street. Between the house and the road was a garden of sorts, an empty lot where tropical vines and shrubs and flowers all stretched and bloomed under the abundant sun. They tossed their heady scent into the warming air, and I caught it, up in the second-floor window where I stood, and I breathed.

There were trees along the road too—great big trees with rounded trunks and generous branches. A few groups of men had gathered under these trees to pass a moment in their shade. The men laughed gently among themselves. Some sat; some stood. They talked, or beamed at one another, or just looked off into the distance. Relaxed. At peace. Unafraid.

I took in all this with a glance. My mind distilled the data and delivered a swift assessment of the facts: *This is a dangerous place.*

The thought came, and it went. As fast as I'd thought those words, I realized with a stab of horror why that particular sentence had formed itself in me. *You only think that because they're Black.*

Black men, standing idly under the window where I slept. Just going about their business, and my mind said, *Danger.*

I was taken aback. I truly hadn't known I felt that way. If I'd seen the same thing back home in America—groups of Black men near me—I might have filtered the scene through another layer of cultural context before drawing a conclusion. It's dangerous here because . . . the back alley, the gang colors, the graffiti, the expressions, the voices, the swaggers. Regardless of whether any of those factors was actually present or actually dangerous (or actually racist), my ability to point to another piece of evidence would have functioned as a means of letting myself off the hook. But in Malawi, all that was stripped away, and there was nothing left but the color of their skin. I knew instantly that it was my reaction to their skin color, and their skin color alone, that had caused me to feel threatened.

And then, I felt exposed. Not by the level of danger—there was none—but by the awareness that something lived in me I did not know I'd welcomed.

Two years later, in September 2001, I enrolled as a graduate student in a one-year Master in Teaching program—the kind where you have to learn how to teach reading, writing, math, social studies, and science, not to mention classroom management, all in a span of months before cranking through your student teaching and qualifying for certification. There was one day devoted to educational inequality. As a means of getting us engaged, the professors gave a simple assignment: Form groups of three, go outside, and talk about your experiences with racism. As we filed out of the classroom and down the hall, I thought about the story I planned to share. I wanted to be real, authentic, vulnerable.

We found a low wall along the edge of the front lawn. I settled myself atop the concrete barrier, wriggling to avoid the branches that poked out from shrubbery just behind me. I listened as my classmate shared the pain of navigating childhood as a person of multiracial heritage. "People were always saying to me, 'What *are* you?'" she recalled with sadness and anger. "Like I wasn't even human."

"I'm so sorry," murmured the blond woman on the other side of me. "That sounds awful."

Then it was my turn. There, on the manicured lawn of an American institute of higher learning, I fumbled for the words to explain what I had grasped that morning in Malawi. "I first realized I was racist when—"

My biracial classmate gasped. She pulled away. Her eyes narrowed in horror.

I stumbled over my words, confused by the disgust on my classmate's face. *I didn't mean . . . but I'm not racist now!* I wanted to say. *I didn't want it or choose it. I didn't even know it was there!* But I didn't say those things. Instead, I rushed through an abbreviated version of my story and clamped my mouth shut. That classmate never looked at me or spoke to me again. And I did not say another word about my own racism—to anyone, ever—for almost two decades.

But the opposite of supremacy is not shame. I could not work my way out of my own ingrained White supremacy while I was feeling shamed into silence. Perhaps I deserved to be shamed; even so, it did not help me heal.

I wanted to try again—to learn to honestly probe the depths of my own heart. In the two decades since that morning in Malawi, and especially since I'd begun walking with Jacob Vanderpool, I had been watching for the racism in my subconscious to reveal itself again. And it had. Not always or often, but enough that I knew it was there and it was real. But I didn't know what to do with it. At one point, I prepared a confessional blog post on the subject, but I couldn't bring myself to press the Publish button. I was too afraid of shame.

Then I attended an online workshop for Christian writers, led by two Black women, Velynn Brown and Chanté Griffin. Throughout the weekend, I was struck by the way the whole thing had such a different center of spiritual gravity than I was used to encountering among White Christians. In the majority-White church, I often found myself navigating between left and right: groups of Christians who were fired up about justice but seemed to doubt the nearness of God, or groups of Christians who focused on friendship with Jesus to the exclusion of any social issue. The space held by Velynn and Chanté in that little workshop was different. I later found my observations articulated in the work of Esau McCaulley: The Black church, he explained, has long been a home for the project of holding vital spirituality together with a focus on social action. Though I hadn't been able to word it quite like that at the time, that's what I noticed there in that online writing workshop.

The weekend included a fifteen-minute consultation where we could ask about any problem we were having in our writing. I signed up eagerly. I knew I needed to get some advice about confession.

Chanté was late to our Zoom breakout room. "I'm so sorry!"

she burst out as her face finally appeared on my screen. "I was out walking, communing with the cows!"

I laughed at the wide-eyed wonder still visible on her face from her morning's adventures. I swallowed the lump that had been building in my throat as I'd sat there waiting for her.

"It's totally fine," I said. "I know we don't have much time left, so I'll jump right in. I wanted to ask you about public confession— specifically when White people confess their own racism." I dropped my eyes to my desk. "I know there's tons of possible problems with it, like I might hurt the feelings of my readers of color. Or maybe I'll focus too much on my own individual stuff and not see my complicity in the larger society? Or maybe I'm only confessing to make myself seem better than other people. Is it centering myself, when I should just be focusing on repairing the harms racism has caused? And yeah, I guess I'm just afraid of the response, like will I be 'canceled,' or will my words be twisted out of context? Or maybe I'm just making a bunch of excuses!"

I inhaled and brought my eyes back up to the screen.

Chanté had a big smile on her face. She was staring almost but not quite into my eyes, the way you do on Zoom. "Sarah," she said, "you have to start from the place of being loved and forgiven by God."

I was startled. I hadn't expected that. I knew that no individual Black person could absolve me, or any of us, of our sins. I'd read Austin Channing Brown's memoir, *I'm Still Here*, in which she described the exhaustion she felt after speaking engagements, when White person after White person would line up to confess racialized sin after racialized sin. "White people really want this to be what reconciliation means," Channing Brown wrote. "A Black person forgiving them for one racist sin." I knew that, and I didn't want that, or I didn't want to want that. I just wanted to figure out whether I ought to be publicly confessing anything at all.

But Chanté wasn't offering me her own forgiveness. She was simply reminding me that I had already been forgiven by God. And in that moment, as I stared through my computer screen at the face of a Black woman several hundred miles away, her eyes still twinkling from her encounter with a bunch of cows, her face became for me the face of Christ. *You are forgiven.*

So here goes. I step into the confessional because I know I am loved and forgiven already, and it is the kindness of God that makes me bold enough to think again. I step into the confessional because looking at Jacob Vanderpool and the White supremacy of the people who surrounded him has forced me to think differently about my own heart. I step into the confessional because I want nothing more than to see our nation healed and I don't know any other way to begin than to raise my hand and go first.

I step into the confessional. I make my confession to Jesus, but I leave the door ajar so you can overhear.

Forgive me, You who slipped into this world wearing brown skin. I have believed the lie that White bodies are more valuable than the bodies of people of color. I did not know I believed this until several years ago when my brother commented, "Did you hear everybody's sharing these nude pictures of Jennifer Lawrence that somebody leaked online?"

I shrugged. My brain had subbed in *Lopez* for *Lawrence,* and I was picturing the Latina singer. "When you're a celebrity, that's sort of what you're signing up for, isn't it?"

Suddenly I remembered who Jennifer Lawrence was. With a jolt, I changed my mind.

"I mean, no!" I felt a sudden, visceral desire to protect the White woman who, I privately thought, looked a little bit like me. "That's terrible!"

And then I realized that in slipping up, my brain had revealed another hidden pocket of subconscious White supremacy. When I believed that my brother's question referred to the ethics of sharing nude photos of an actress of color, I didn't bother to assign much mental energy to the dilemma. It was fine. Celebrity bodies were sort of public already, weren't they? But when I realized he was asking about a White actress, my indignation flared. *Her* body doesn't belong to *them!*

Either position could be argued, I suppose: that celebrities have somehow given consent to public viewing simply by becoming celebrities or that everyone deserves to be protected from paparazzi. If I hadn't confused the two Jennifers, I would have stuck to one position or the other. Only when I made a mistake and compared my two conclusions side by side did I become aware that there was a racial calculus at play. Only then could I learn of my own double standard. My own implicit bias. My own White supremacy.

How did I come to believe that the body of a woman of color was available for public scrutiny when I also apparently believed that the body of a White woman belongs only to herself? Why did I assign less value to the woman of color than to the woman who looked like me? *I* never went to a slave market, running my eyes up and down the naked flesh of other human beings, calculating the degree of physical strain they could endure on my behalf. *I* never opened another woman's mouth to count her teeth, squeezed her muscles to assess her strength, yanked her hair to judge her health. *I* never stripped anyone for a whipping. *I* never wound my way from the church to the public square on a Sunday morning after the worship service let out, pushed along by a crowd eager to see the bodies hanging in the breeze. *I* never purchased a lynching postcard as a souvenir. But my ancestors did. *My ancestors did.* My ancestors did, and how could it surprise me that after all that, some vestige of their White supremacy lived on in my own subconscious?

This implicit preference for White bodies worms its way into so many facets of our lives. I recently read the results of a study revealing that Black babies are less likely to die when they are delivered into the hands of Black obstetricians. This study strips away all the other factors we like to point to when comparing child mortality rates by race—the health of the mother, access to prenatal care, socioeconomic status—and locates one possible part of the problem as simply the "spontaneous bias" of some White doctors themselves. Let's not imagine that such doctors are intentional in their neglect. But what a heartbreak if even a handful of obstetricians find themselves, in the frantic moments following a small but infinitely tragic number of births, captive to some subconscious calculus that leaves more Black babies dead.

Lord, have mercy.

. . .

Forgive me, You who walked among us in humility, poverty, and gentleness. I have exercised the lie that I possess some false authority over those whose skin is darker than mine. Years ago, my husband and I went to see the movie *The Passion of the Christ* in the theater. The film is, arguably, maudlin and overdone, but I was trying to take it seriously. My spiritual contemplation was interrupted, however, by loud, ongoing laughter from some people in the back.

I assumed the noise came from a group of teenagers. I was a middle school English teacher at the time, practiced in wresting some kind of control over rowdy kids. As the interruption continued, I grew increasingly irritated. Finally, I jumped out of my seat and strode across the darkened theater, rehearsing my speech as I went.

When I reached the source of the commotion, I was surprised to find myself face-to-face with a group of Black women, all at least ten to twenty years older than I was. But still, I launched into the angry-middle-school-teacher rant I'd been preparing as I marched across the theater. *"You all need to be quiet!"* I half shrieked.

Later, I told myself that I just didn't have time to summon the respect I would have ordinarily employed when interacting with people older than me. (The question of why I thought respect was appropriate for older and not younger people is a subject for another day.) But I wonder now: If the group had been White, would I have found a last-second way to switch direction? To turn my visit to their row into a polite request instead of a shrill demand? I hate to acknowledge it, but I think I would have.

Another time, my false authority was much more premeditated. In my early twenties, I belonged to a Bible study with chapters all over the world. Every chapter followed the same clear hierarchy: A teaching leader would stand in the pulpit and deliver a lecture, and discussion leaders would shepherd small-group conversations. A centralized board of directors visited each chapter annually, encouraging them to follow all the rules that had been developed, from exactly how many hymns to sing to exactly what size name tags to provide. My mother had belonged to this Bible study my entire life, and I had been attending it since early college. I knew the organization's rules and layers of authority, and I respected them.

When I moved to Seattle just after college, I switched from a suburban, mostly White chapter of the Bible study to an urban, mostly Black chapter. The White teaching leader of the suburban group had always worn her name tag in the pulpit, but the Black teaching leader of the urban group never did. It was such a small thing, but it rankled me. I was not part of the group's leadership structure at all, but every week I sat in the pew and thought about why she wasn't wearing her name tag like she was supposed to. Finally, one day I approached her about it.

"I think you're supposed to be wearing a name tag," I said. I was twenty-two years old, and this woman was in her forties or fifties and at least two levels of authority above me in the structure of the organization. I don't believe I ever would have approached a White teaching leader in this way. What in the world gave me the gall to walk up to a Black leader and complain about something so stupid as wearing a name tag?

She looked at me. "The board told me not to wear it," she finally replied. "Because of the glare from the overhead lights in this church's sanctuary."

"Oh." I felt embarrassed, and I shuffled back to my seat.

How did I come to believe that I had the right to correct a woman who had been given express authority over me? That I had the right to shush a group of older women like they were a bunch of kids? *I* never sat in a legislative body and debated which people groups deserved the full stature of humanity and which did not. *I* never presided over a court case and decided whose testimony was worth hearing and whose was not; whose presence in the community was worth defending and whose was not. But I grew up in a society founded on those debates and decisions.

This, I think, is why the Ten Commandments warn that the sin of the parents will be visited on the third and fourth generation of their children. I don't read it as an arbitrary punishment but more as an observation of fact: Sin has consequences. A society that colludes to viciously oppress a group of people, century after century, is going to hear the echoes of that sin for a very long time.

Lord, have mercy.

Forgive me, You who gave Yourself away, allowing Your life to be taken for our sakes on the cross. I have believed the lie that everything must center on me. This lie has been the hardest to ferret out. Of course my life centers on me: I look at the world through my own eyes, hear the world through my own ears. We are all the protagonists of our own stories. But can I see the way I put my own self above others, even subtly? It's difficult. Sometimes gaining an awareness of our own subconscious biases requires a trip to the realm of our sleeping dreams.

Shortly after George Floyd's death in the summer of 2020, my friend Malika Lee organized a series of small-group encounters designed to get people talking about the way racism (or sexism, or classism) appeared in their sleeping dreams. Malika based her idea for these groups on a scene from the book *The Wisdom of Your Dreams,* in which author Jeremy Taylor described how a group of well-intentioned White volunteers could not manage to effectively come alongside a Black community until they started analyzing the racialized bogeymen who appeared in their sleeping dreams.

I agreed to lead a group, even though I was a little skeptical of the project—it felt a bit woo-woo to me—and I wasn't entirely clear on how the conversations were supposed to flow. But I was trying to follow Black leadership, and Malika was one of the only Black people I knew "in real life" who was leading me anywhere. Unsurprisingly, given my ambivalence, my group fell apart after just a few sessions. Perhaps the whole experience is an example of my unwillingness to allow myself to be truly led. But several weeks of focusing on remembering my dreams—along with the intention of discovering racism there—did lead to an unexpected revelation.

I had a dream that I was at an all-you-can-eat buffet, a long line of hot dishes stretching out before me. But as I started toward the food, I noticed there was a Black man in line ahead of me. "Get out of my way!" dream-me barked, shoving the man roughly aside. "You don't deserve to be here!"

I woke up deeply troubled. Why was *that* inside me? I would never do that . . . would I? I told the other White women in my group, but they shrugged it off. "Sometimes we dream really yucky things," one said. "Just forget about it."

But I couldn't forget. The dream popped into my mind at different times, especially in the grocery store whenever I rounded the end of an aisle and found someone else moving toward the exact spot where I wanted to go. I had never paid much attention to the choreography of the dance of shopping carts. But now, with my dream in mind, I realized that a minute calculation had been taking place. I would pull my cart back for other White shoppers. But I pushed ahead when I met shoppers of color. The difference was measured in millimeters and half seconds: who I saw, who I didn't see; when I nodded and stopped; when I waved and kept rolling. But it was there.

Shortly afterward, my friend Robert Monson posted on Twitter, "This might seem small . . . Black people . . . do y'all notice people don't move out of our way in the grocery store or is that my imagination?" As of the last time I checked, 952 people had liked the comment, 198 people retweeted it, and 243 responded. *Yes,* other Black people said. *Yes, we see this. Yes, we experience it.*

I have a White friend who believes that a hyper-focus on racism has led Black people to see racism where it doesn't exist. "If you tell them that racism is happening, of course they're going to see it all over the place," she insists. "It's not good for them."

But I don't think that's what's happening at all. I think a reverse kind of magic has taken place: We, White people, are the ones who've told ourselves that our own racism doesn't exist. We've convinced ourselves not to see what our own bodies and minds are doing. We center ourselves, pushing our own selves forward. And it's not good for anybody.

Lord, have mercy.

These might seem like small confessions. An overly forceful movie-theater shush. A misunderstanding about a name tag. A mix-up between two celebrities. An unyielded inch in the grocery store. For me, they represent isolated incidents sprinkled seemingly infrequently across the long years of my life.

But how would it feel to be the recipient of these oversteps all day, every day? Austin Channing Brown described a typical day in the life of a Black woman working in a professional, mostly White setting.

8:55 A.M.: . . . I am asked three times if I need help finding the outreach center. . . . *The message: I am a Black woman, so I must be poor and in need of help.*

8:58 A.M.: . . . She reaches out to touch my hair. . . . *The message: I am different, exotic. Anyone should have the right to my body.*

9:58 A.M.: . . . [My supervisor] tells me she received a note saying that I made someone uncomfortable. . . . *The message: I am responsible for the feelings of white people.*

10:05 A.M.: I attempt to respond, but before I can finish, my supervisor asks if I don't mind changing my tone a bit. . . .

The message: My tone will be interpreted as angry, even if I'm just feeling hurt or misunderstood.

The day goes on, with minor incident stacking upon minor incident, until Channing Brown concluded, "It's difficult to express how these incidents accumulate, making you feel undervalued, unappreciated, and ultimately expendable."

For me, a White woman traveling in mostly White circles, my interactions with people of color are few enough already. The interactions that rise to the level of my being consciously aware of their awkward racist undertones are so infrequent I can tally them up in a few pages. For a person of color—whose survival instincts, after generations of living among White people, have been keenly honed to be sensitive to our every flicker—just getting through the day can feel like a bombardment.

Forgive us, Lord.

The first time I confessed all this, I was on a silent spiritual retreat on Washington's Olympic Peninsula. I did not write it down for an audience; I wrote it down for Jesus. I sat in my tiny bedroom in the retreat center where I was staying and wrote across pages and pages of my prayer journal. In the past, shame had prevented me from truly seeing my sin; before each glimpse could fully surface, I'd stuffed it back down to fester below the reaches of my conscious mind once again. But forgiveness now quieted my shame, giving me space to truly examine and lament. By the time I was done, tears were streaming down my face.

Something happens in the confessional. I mean "confessional" here metaphorically, for I am not Roman Catholic and have never set foot in a wooden confession box. But whether our confessional is a prayer journal, or a conversation with a trusted friend, or a spot where we kneel on our bedroom floor, I believe that in those holy spaces, a real spiritual transaction takes place. It is not that we are forgiven there, for we were forgiven before we even began to confess. What happens in the confessional is that sin loses its power over us. It is a marvelous mystery that the only way to release our shame is to get honest about our sin. The only way to receive the abundant love of God is to make space for it in our contrite hearts. The only way to begin to work toward repair is first to acknowledge what is broken.

When I tried to confess my sin to my classmates in my teaching program, I got silenced by shame, and it took me twenty years to get unstuck. "Shame can be a catalyst and a teacher," wrote myisha t hill, "but only if we move through it. Then, we can fail our way forward to heal." Somehow, Chanté Griffin's reminder to me of God's love became an invitation to keep moving. To step into the confessional and fail my way forward once again.

After I wrote out my confession in the silent-retreat center, I walked down to a little beachfront on a nearby inlet. I perched on a driftwood log and stared out across the water. The branches of the giant cedar trees on the opposite shore swayed gently in the breeze. An osprey looped above me, watching for his chance to dive. My breathing steadied and the tears on my cheeks dried. It occurred to me then that the opposite of supremacy is not shame; it is shalom.

Shalom: the Hebrew concept of wholeness. Everything in its place. Not superior or inferior. Not pumped up with pride or weighed down with shame. At peace. Shalom.

What parents and lawmakers who try to forbid the teaching of our nation's racist history don't seem to understand is that confronting the truth about our past—and ourselves—is not what makes us feel shame. Shame is already present. When we choose to keep silent instead of confronting those truths, shame only grows. When we bring the truth about ourselves into the light of God's love, that is when we become free.

I want to be clear that the primary purpose of confession is not simply making ourselves feel better. What we want—what God wants for us—is to do better. To be better. For beauty and justice and truth to flourish in all the places where ugliness and unfairness and lies have reigned. Once that work has begun in the depths of our own hearts, we must learn to carry it to every corner of this bruised and weary planet. But it is a fundamental law of the universe that only loved people can love. Only by meeting the forgiving gaze of the God who is Love can we embark on the work of making things right. What a mercy to discover that when that gaze sets us free—to *do* better and to *be* better—it *feels* better too.

I once watched a video online of a teacher speaking at the 2019 Teacher of the Year conference. Her name was Leigh Ann Erickson, and she was a White English teacher who taught African American literature to classes of mostly White high school students in Iowa. In her lecture, Erickson described the psychological stretching her students experienced when she helped them understand the complex history of race in this country. Sometimes it was hard for them to face up to the reality of our nation's past. But Erickson knew exactly why she pushed her White students to grapple with this history. "This is for their joy," she insisted, her voice rising with emotion. "This is for their joy."

Somehow, as I sat on the beach and watched the osprey plunge into the sea, I knew exactly what she meant.

Chapter Seven

The Pastor

Portrait of Ezra Fisher, circa 1845.
From *Baptist Annals of Oregon*.

On the morning of August 25, 1851, the trial began.

First, Vanderpool's attorney, Amory Holbrook, mounted his defense. Vanderpool himself would not take the stand, perhaps because Holbrook knew that his client's testimony, like Kezika's, would be inadmissible. It is impossible to know how Holbrook felt about the case. He was no stranger to racially charged cases; he himself had prosecuted the five Cayuse men who'd been hanged for the Whitman killings the year before. But this time, on the other side of the courtroom, Holbrook made a serious attempt at defense. He began by demanding Vanderpool's release, because "the alleged statute of this territory by virtue of which he is arrested is in all respects unconstitutional and inconsistent with the laws and the Constitution of the United States."

The alleged statute . . . is in all respects unconstitutional. That should have been the end of it. In the words of her Constitution, America had promised her people justice, tranquility, and the blessings of liberty. The Exclusion Law was unconstitutional. What more did anyone need to hear?

Outside the wooden courthouse, Oregon City's residents were going about their ordinary Monday mornings. On one end of Main Street, the newspaper printer at the *Statesman* office was laying out the typeset for the next day's edition. Elsewhere on Main Street, the "butter, old" and "butter, fresh" salesmen were beginning to hawk their wares. And at the other end of Main Street, Ezra Fisher—pastor of the Oregon City Baptist Church, founding professor of Oregon City College, and a distant relative of my own— was probably working to prepare for another school year teaching Oregon's first crop of college students.

When my husband was in seminary, my grandmother wanted to know if he'd ever heard of her theologically famous cousin—her second cousin once removed, to be exact: Kenneth

Scott Latourette. Yale University Divinity School's Sterling Professor of Missions and Oriental History and author of the seven-volume *A History of the Expansion of Christianity* and the relatively slimmer 1,500-page *A History of Christianity.* "I have!" my husband replied, and it wasn't just to appease her. He had recently landed a graduate student position as registrar of the American Society of Missiology. Apparently, my distant cousin had essentially founded their entire branch of theology.

And in 1916, before he went to Yale or penned his weighty tomes, Kenneth Scott Latourette had collated, for publication in the *Oregon Historical Quarterly,* the correspondence of his great-grandfather, the pioneer, pastor, and professor Ezra Fisher.

The significance of all this was lost on me at the time, of course. I hadn't heard of Jacob Vanderpool back then, much less Ezra Fisher. When I found out that my second cousin four times removed had founded a branch of theology, I shrugged. I never asked my grandmother about her semi-famous cousin. She'd probably never asked him about his semi-famous great-grandfather. So, a decade and a half after my grandmother's conversation with my husband, when I finally became interested in the goings-on of 1851 Oregon City and discovered that someone in my family had actually lived there then, the thin line that connected me to that place in that time had already been nearly erased. My grandmother was gone. Her cousin Kenneth Scott Latourette was long gone. His great-grandfather Ezra Fisher had been gone longer still. If I wanted to follow the trail that connected me to my . . . great-great-great-great-uncle's father-in-law? . . . I would have to find it myself.

A mory Holbrook did not rest his case with the general uncon-
stitutionality of Vanderpool's arrest. He went on to specifically argue that the indictment violated article 4, section 2 of the
Constitution of the United States; the Fifth, Sixth, and Eighth
Amendments of the Constitution of the United States; and the Second and Sixth Articles of the Northwest Ordinance.

As I peered at the handwritten scratches in the mimeographs I'd
hastily snapped pictures of when I'd visited the Special Collections
Library, I felt a bit lost in the weeds of all this legal maneuvering.
So I decided to reach out to a cousin of my own.

My cousin Peter holds degrees in history, international human
rights, and law, and I could not imagine a more perfect combina-
tion of expertise to help me make sense of the Vanderpool trial.
Peter graciously agreed to look at the documents, and I sent them
over. On lunch break from his new job clerking for a family court
judge in Delaware, Peter emailed to call my attention to Holbrook's second line of argument. After bringing up all the amendments and articles violated by Vanderpool's arrest, the defense
attorney had said this: "In the second place, that the complaint and
affidavit are insufficient, because it does not appear therefrom that
he is not, in and by said alleged law, even if it be adjudged constitutional, one of the persons permitted to remain."

"How do you read that?" Peter asked me.

"I'm not a lawyer," I wrote back.

"But you are an English specialist," he replied.

I'm not sure I'd consider a creative writing degree evidence of specialism in much of anything, but I pondered the sentence for a while. *It does not appear that he is* not *one of the persons permitted to remain*. In other words, he might be one of the persons *permitted* to remain.

"Are they arguing that he might be White?" Peter asked.

"Maybe," I wrote back. "Or are they trying to put the burden of proof for Vanderpool's race on the prosecution?"

Was Vanderpool's status as "mulatto" not readily apparent? Who gets to judge whether any one of us is or is not a member of this or that race, anyway?

The term *mulatto* originally referred to a person with one parent of European descent and one of African. Later, it expanded to include the descendants of those original "mulattos." Other terms cropped up as well: a *quadroon* was a person with one grandparent of African descent; an *octoroon*, a person with one Black great-grandparent. (Homer Plessy—whose 1896 U.S. Supreme Court case *Plessy v. Ferguson*, when he lost it, established the legal validity of segregation in America for the next sixty-eight years—was an octoroon.) Eventually, the "one-drop rule" was developed. Anyone with any degree of African ancestry was considered Black, regardless of how far back in the genealogy that African ancestor had lived or how dark or pale the color of their descendant's skin. The nineteenth-century jurists did not know, of course, that we all hail from Africa.

Jacob Vanderpool was a "mulatto" from the West Indies, where White men had been preying on Black women and their daughters for centuries. Some of the descendants of those unions were light-skinned enough to pass for White. So, when Holbrook argued "it does not appear" that Vanderpool was "not . . . one of the persons permitted to remain," he might have been arguing that Vanderpool looked mostly White.

But White supremacy in nineteenth-century America was not primarily concerned with appearances; it was primarily concerned with power. Ultimately, it didn't matter whether Jacob Vanderpool appeared to be one of the persons permitted to remain or not.

In my search for my distant relative Ezra Fisher, I began with his letters. I ordered a print copy of *Correspondence of the Reverend Ezra Fisher* off Amazon from a publisher called Forgotten Books. When it arrived, I discovered that the publisher had simply stuck photocopies of multiple full editions of the *Oregon Historical Quarterly* together in one binding. Fisher's letters were scattered across several volumes, among works by 1916 historians with titles like "The Indian of the Northwest" and "Some Documentary Records of Slavery in Oregon." Fisher had written most of his letters to the correspondence secretary of the American Baptist Home Missionary Society, or "Cor. Sec. A. B. H. M. Soc.," as he abbreviated it. The letters in the Forgotten Books reprint spanned the years 1847 to 1852.

I would later learn that Ezra Fisher was born in Massachusetts in the first week of the nineteenth century. His career as a Baptist missionary pastor took him to the edge of the American West with every expansion of the nation's frontier: Indiana, Illinois, Iowa.

Eventually, in 1845, Fisher packed up his wife and four children and made the overland journey to Oregon. When they arrived, Dr. John McLoughlin supplied the family with transportation and supplies. Although they settled first in Astoria, Fisher did not succeed in founding a church there. But he did manage to establish the first Baptist meetinghouse west of the Rocky Mountains in Oregon City in 1847, and the family moved full-time to Oregon City in 1849, the year before Jacob Vanderpool arrived.

It was clear to me, as I read through his letters, that Ezra Fisher was a devout man of God. He cared deeply for the people of Oregon and for the cause of Christ. But as I scanned the splotchy font of the reprinted pages, I wondered whether Fisher had cared at all about his neighbor Jacob Vanderpool. I did not wish to condemn my ancestor; I only wanted to understand what role he had played, or not played, in the case that would make history books.

In the correspondence of Reverend Ezra Fisher, I found no mention of Jacob Vanderpool. Fisher did spill a lot of ink accounting for his time. A typical list declares that since his last letter, he had

> preached 13 sermons; delivered two lectures; attended one
> prayer-meeting; one covenant meeting; visited religiously
> 20 families and 12 individuals; visited no common schools;
> baptized none; obtained no signatures to the temperance
> pledge; neither assisted at the organization of a church nor
> the ordination of a minister; have taught regularly a Bible
> class of 10 scholars, except four Sabbaths of my absence;
> distributed about 500 pages of tracts, 10 Bibles and 20 Testa-

ments; traveled 450 miles to and from my appointments; received no person either by letter or experience; no cases of conversion in the field of my labor; no young men preparing for the ministry.

Fisher was a busy man, devoted to his cause. He also spent a lot of time worrying about the future of Oregon. "Everything is to be done," he wrote, encouraging the Home Missionary Board to send more church workers west, "if this part of the country is to be saved from the reign of idolatry, the tyranny of skepticism and the dominion of the Beast." Elsewhere, he wrote, "If I have one object for which I desire to live more than all others, it is to see the cause for which Christ impoverished himself making the people of Oregon rich."

But more immediate riches would come from another source. When news of the California Gold Rush first reached him, Fisher imagined a spiritual harvest. The miners included "some from China" and "almost every nation in Europe," he had heard: "What a point then is San Francisco for the men of God to take with Bibles and devotional books and tracts, sending them as upon the wings of the wind!" But when Fisher traveled to California, the reality of living with heathens dampened his evangelistic zeal. "Nothing would induce me to spend three or four months in the midst of profane swearing, drunkenness, gambling, and Sabbath breaking," he wrote from California, "but the hope of providing for my dear family." Fisher returned north as soon as possible, with "$1000 worth of gold" and "an abiding conviction of the duty I owe to the cause of Christ in Oregon."

In 1850, Reverend Fisher added teaching and school administration to his list of duties. "At this period in my life I have not the most distant desire to engage in teaching," Fisher wrote to his faraway correspondent, but "a conviction of duty . . . has brought me . . . to this employment." The Oregon settlers who valued higher education had realized that sending their children back east for school would be impractical. Therefore, a committee had elected Ezra Fisher to head the first institute of higher education west of the Rocky Mountains. For a couple of years, until John McLoughlin donated a separate building, Ezra Fisher's Oregon City College met inside his church. "All kinds of labor are richly rewarded," Fisher lamented in the early months of his new endeavor, "except that of preachers and teachers."

Another recurrent theme in Fisher's letters was his deep longing for more books. Books hadn't made the cut in most of the Oregon Trail oxcarts, and the pastor/professor missed them sorely. His regular lament for books reads like a series of messages in a bottle penned by a marooned sailor slowly running out of some indispensable supply. "We shall much need classical books," Fisher wrote at the outset of his college's founding. "We want a small, well selected library," he wrote months later. Months after that: "Our whole territory is materially suffering for want of school books now." And later still: "We are now out of school books."

Yet another anxiety was the fact that Fisher's daughter Lucy was putting in too many hours helping him at the school. Over and over, he complained to the board that his daughter "devotes most of her time" to teaching at the college.

In September 1851, the same month Jacob Vanderpool would be

ordered to leave Oregon, Ezra Fisher solved both his book trou-
bles and his concerns for his daughter at a stroke: He married Lucy
to my great-great-great-grandfather's brother, Lyman D. C. Latourette, the first bookseller on the West Coast.

Thousands of words flowed from Reverend Ezra Fisher's pen
during this time. He discussed his work, his neighbors, his financial needs, the exact sizes of the boots and clothing each member of
his family required—but nothing about race, politics, Oregon's
exclusion laws, or the one neighbor who had not been met with the
same welcome the Fishers had received when they arrived in Oregon.

On August 8, 1851, two and a half weeks before the trial that
would exile his African American neighbor from the Territory he
longed to influence for Christ, Ezra Fisher wrote, "Unless we are
visited with the outpourings of the spirit from on high, we are a
ruined people in Oregon."

In his next letter, dated a week after the Vanderpool trial, Fisher
said, "Religious matters in the Territory remain much as they were
when I last wrote."

The prosecution did not answer any of the defense's arguments. Their objective seemed to be to establish that Jacob
Vanderpool had arrived in Oregon after September 21, 1849, so his
presence in the state had not been grandfathered in. A Captain
Chandler claimed to have seen Jacob Vanderpool in Philadelphia
two years ago last March. A Mr. Harrison stated, "I don't know

when Jacob came in the country. I heard him say that he came here last August. My impression is that he was born in the West India Islands."

And with that, the prosecution brought its argument to rest.

I wondered whether, on the night of August 25—after the evidence had been heard, but before the verdict had been rendered— when Theophilus Magruder and Thomas Nelson walked home together from the courthouse, eagerly anticipating their clean sheets and fried beefsteaks, they had passed Ezra Fisher on the street.

Ezra Fisher spoke so many words—in Oregon's pulpits Sunday after Sunday and in its classrooms Monday through Friday. But the vast majority of those words were never captured at all. Was it fair, then, for me to charge my ancestor with silence on the topic of race when I could not verify whether he had, in fact, said something I could simply no longer hear? I hardly knew what my parents' and grandparents' lives consisted of, much less the lives of the forebears I never met. What if Fisher preached eloquent sermons about Jacob Vanderpool's plight every week all summer and they simply hadn't been handed down? I decided to keep looking.

I turned first to the Oregon City Baptist Church. The present building isn't the original one, and it's no longer located in the same place, but the congregation traces its lineage all the way back to the church Ezra Fisher founded in 1847. Today, the church uses the tagline "Small. Slow. Weird."

I sent an email. True to their tagline, the response was not immediate. But a few weeks later, I received an invitation to come poke around in the church archives.

When I arrived, I was greeted by the pastor's wife, a middle school teacher who helped run the church office during the summer. She and her husband were the church's only employees. I loved them both immediately. Church ministry can be a lonely thing, and as a pastor's wife myself, I felt an instant kinship. After I'd been digging through files for a couple of hours, they bought me a burrito and we sat in the church office and talked about God and America and history and the church and where the Spirit might now be blowing.

After lunch, the pastor unlocked the sanctuary so I could see the stained glass windows that bore my family members' names. "In Memory of Dr. Ruth Latourette Eaton," said one; "In Memory of Mr. & Mrs. D. C. Latourette," said another. I wasn't sure who Dr. Ruth was, but Mr. D. C., I knew. He was my first cousin four times removed and father of the famous theologian Kenneth Scott. I stood in the rose-lit sanctuary and wondered what it had been like for my distant cousin Kenneth, who literally wrote the book on the history of Christianity, to grow up in this church. It probably hadn't referred to itself as small, slow, and weird at the time.

Most of that day I spent tucked into a room so small only one person could enter. The pastor unlocked it for me and then gestured vaguely. "I can't fit in there with you," he said. "Just take a look and see what you can find. Watch out for the broken glass on the upper shelves."

Someone had stuffed a row of metal filing cabinets into what was essentially a narrow closet. There wasn't room to both stand in front of a filing cabinet and open it at the same time; I had to stand next to the one I wanted and work sideways. Inside each drawer, manila folders were labeled by name or year. There was a folder on Ezra Fisher, a folder on each of several Latourettes, and a folder on the year 1851.

What I wanted to know was whether Ezra Fisher had ever preached or spoken about the Jacob Vanderpool case. In a town of nine hundred, he must have known it was happening. He'd probably passed Vanderpool on the street a hundred times. Both had lived and worked on Main Street—at most, a half a mile apart. And though Ezra Fisher hadn't been in the courtroom when Thomas Nelson handed down his verdict, he must have heard about it after the fact.

On August 26, 1851, Thomas Nelson had decreed the following:

> In the matter of the Complaint of Theophilus Magruder against Jacob Vanderpool a mulatto.
>
> The above-named Jacob Vanderpool, having been brought before me on a warrant based upon the complaint of the above named Theophilus Magruder, and I being satisfied, that the said Jacob Vanderpool is a mulatto, and that he is remaining in the territory of Oregon contrary to the statutes and laws of the territory. I therefore order that the said Jacob Vanderpool remove from the said territory within thirty days from and after the service of this order. The said order to be served by showing to the said Jacob this original and at the same time delivering to him a true copy of the same.
>
> 26 August, 1851
> Thomas Nelson
> Chief Justice
> For the territory of Oregon

If Ezra Fisher had remarked upon that verdict from his pulpit, I found no evidence in the basement of the Oregon City Baptist Church. In the church's files, I found only silence.

There were meeting minutes and sermon notes, faded photographs and summaries penned by diligent church historians. But the only direct reference to race that I could find in those filing cabinets was a line in an account Ezra Fisher's son had written, decades afterward, about their time in Independence, Missouri, at the outset of their journey along the Oregon Trail. "There was a high bank of clay along the river," he wrote, "and on it I saw every day Indian men and women seated with their feet hanging over the water, apparently in deep meditation, but probably with minds entirely vacant."

Next, I tried Linfield University. Linfield is located in McMinnville, some forty miles away, but it traces its roots to Oregon City College. "Traces its roots" means, in this case, that when the latter closed its doors in 1888, its trustees gave a bell, some books, and the proceeds of the sale of their property to what would eventually become Linfield. Evidently, Oregon City College had also donated some papers by and about their founder, Ezra Fisher. When I emailed Rich Schmidt, Linfield's Director of Archives and Resource Sharing, he invited me to come take a look.

At 9:45 A.M. on a Friday in September, the university library was nearly empty, but the archive room showed signs of life. Though most of its dozen or so desks were devoid of human occupants, they were loaded with half-written papers and half-read books. The walls were covered with hand-painted murals of familiar characters: Snow White and the Seven Dwarfs, Dora the Explorer and friends. The faces in the murals had been replaced with goofy photographs of, I guessed, the students and staff who worked in this room. Around the edges of the murals, celebrities grinned from what appeared to be every American Library Association READ poster ever made. Two hip-high plastic M&M's characters filled with cellophane stood guard near the door. It was an entirely different vibe from the archive closet at the Oregon City Baptist Church.

I gently moved a fleece blanket out of the chair where Rich directed me to sit, under the steady gaze of a tousled Orlando Bloom clutching a copy of *The Lord of the Rings*. Rich had pulled the relevant files for me already, and they were waiting there on a desk that had been otherwise mostly cleared. "Only one rule," Rich said as he returned to his office. "No ink. Only pencils."

As I flipped through original family letters and sheafs of sermon notes, one of the most exciting things I found in the Linfield archive room was a complete copy of *Correspondence of the Reverend Ezra Fisher*, all in one binding. It had been signed by my grandmother's cousin: "To the Linfield College Library with the compliments of Kenneth S. Latourette, 1904." And it included a preface, written by Kenneth Scott himself, that I had not seen in the Forgotten Books edition.

One paragraph came close to giving me the information I sought:

> Ezra Fisher was a strong anti-slavery man. As time went on
> he found himself in a church and association whose mem-

bers were largely from southern states. For the sake of harmony, his policy at first was to say little.

I had guessed right, it seemed, about Fisher's response to the issue of race in Oregon. Even though he was strongly anti-slavery, "at first"—a time period that surely included the summer of 1851—his policy was "to say little."

The archives of the Oregon City Baptist Church, it seemed, were silent on purpose.

Kenneth Scott Latourette continued:

> But as the slavery question grew larger and Oregon was threatened with admission as a slave state, he felt that it was no time for silence. In public and privately he exerted his influence to the utmost against slavery. When the adoption of a Constitution was before the people, his fight was a valiant one. . . . Few awaited the returns of Nov. 9, 1857, with more anxiety of mind than Ezra Fisher, and none was made more glad by Oregon's decision.

I was relieved to find out that Ezra Fisher had eventually found his voice. Glad that he had railed against slavery in Oregon. But how had he felt about the exclusion laws? The two clauses had been bundled together on that November 1857 ballot: Should Oregon, with its new statehood, allow slavery? And should free Blacks be allowed to live among us? Latourette didn't say, but it seemed unlikely to me that if Fisher had fought against the exclusion laws as hard as he had fought against slavery, he would have been the gladdest man in Oregon when the results of the election were returned. His gladness was a clue, perhaps, that Ezra Fisher had probably voted with the majority of Oregon's citizens. Oregon would be the nation's only anti-slavery *and* officially anti-Black state. Apparently, exclusion, when compared with slavery, felt like a far less serious sin.

Ezra Fisher was a product of his time. Even Abraham Lincoln, the Great Emancipator, said in a speech in 1858, "I am not, nor have ever been, in favor of bringing about in any way the social and political equality of the black and white races."

In any case, whatever Ezra Fisher had or had not said in his pulpit or in his classroom, it had not changed the outcome of Jacob Vanderpool's case. Other men, later convicted of breaking Oregon's exclusion law, were saved from exile by the intervention of their White neighbors. But after Thomas Nelson rendered his August 26 verdict, it was the silence of my own family members that left Jacob Vanderpool to his fate. .

Chapter Eight

From Silence to Self-Disclosure

The American church has yielded the prophetic voice because it has not spoken a historical and theological truth.

—Mark Charles, *Unsettling Truths*

Perhaps it seems as though Ezra Fisher—and his son-in-law Lyman D. C. Latourette—had little to do with Jacob Vanderpool. Ezra Fisher did not found the town that would choose Whiteness as its primary condition of residency, or preside over it as mayor; John McLoughlin did that. Ezra Fisher did not haul Jacob Vanderpool to court just to eliminate a business competitor; Theophilus Magruder did that. Ezra Fisher did not pronounce Jacob Vanderpool guilty of the crime of being Black and impose a sentence of exile; Thomas Nelson did that. Ezra Fisher simply lived there. He even fought, later, *against* slavery in Oregon. What more could he, or Lyman, have done for Jacob Vanderpool?

Jemar Tisby recounted, at the beginning of his book *The Color of Compromise: The Truth About the American Church's Complicity in Racism,* the story of four young Black girls who were killed in 1963 when a bomb went off in their Baptist church in Birmingham, Alabama. At their funeral three days later, a White lawyer named Charles Morgan, Jr., stood and addressed the crowd:

> Who did it? Who threw that bomb? Was it a Negro or a white? The answer should be, "We all did it." Every last one of us is condemned for that crime and the bombing before it and a decade ago. We all did it.

"All the city's white residents," wrote Tisby, "were complicit in allowing an environment of hatred and racism to persist."

Ezra Fisher had not written Oregon's exclusion laws, or filed the lawsuit, or heard the case. But he was a man of influence and standing in Oregon City. He had founded the first Baptist church west of the Rocky Mountains *and* the first college west of them. He taught and preached to Oregon City's residents six days a week. And when Oregon City turned on one of their own, Ezra Fisher remained silent.

"We will have to repent in this generation," wrote Martin Luther King, Jr., from a Birmingham jail just five months before four of that city's youngest citizens were killed by the bomb hurled into their church, "not merely for the vitriolic words and actions of the bad people but for the appalling silence of the good people."

The other thing I found in the Linfield archives was an account Kenneth Scott Latourette wrote in 1962—six years before his death, nine years after the birth of my mother—recalling his boyhood in Oregon City. In it, he reminisced about his grandfather's original homestead. "One of the best farms in Clackamas County," Latourette recalled. "On the land had been a small Indian village and burying ground. For many years two deep holes on back fields remained, dug by the Indians for their sweat baths."

I couldn't believe that in my own mother's lifetime, a family member had still been alive who could clearly recall that our family's property had supplanted a small Indian village and burying ground, complete with sweat baths.

I decided it was time to connect with my Latourette cousins.

A quick online search turned up a website for a recurring family reunion. A Contact link produced an email address. Hours later, I was on the phone with a distant relative.

"Whose daughter are you?" the man on the other end of the line asked me. "Oh, Patty's granddaughter. Sure, sure. I remember her." My grandmother and her sister had attended the Latourette reunions years ago.

"I'm investigating our ancestors," I explained, "and I was wondering if you might have any family documents."

"Oh, we'll have to get you out to the estate," my distant cousin replied. "The property is quite stunning. Been in the family for generations. As for documents, well, I do have a book here at the office. Did you say you were in the area?"

And so I pulled up, a few days later, to a large house tucked into a residential block full of other large houses just a few streets over from Portland's downtown skyscrapers. The house was a newer build than its neighbors and just as magisterial.

"Did you say this was your office?" I asked when my cousin, a spry man in his seventies, came to the door.

"Oh, I owned the property, so I had to put a house on it," he replied. "Resale values, you know."

I nodded and raised my eyebrows in a look of what I hoped approximated appreciation.

"I inherited all of the furniture from my grandmother," he went on, waving at a pair of living rooms, both impeccably decked out in high-end mid-century modern. I smiled vaguely at a chartreuse sofa.

We trooped up to the third floor, where a desk piled with papers stood in the center of a skylit room. "It's just a wonderful family, as I'm sure you've discovered," my cousin said as he rummaged through a closet in the corner of his office. "Such a tremendous heritage. The French Latourettes still own a castle, you know. They were tremendously interested to meet us when we visited. 'Our American cousins!' they said, and they invited us for a lovely meal. Oh, here we are!"

He produced a manila folder containing a stack of yellowed papers and solemnly passed it over. "I'm going to trust you with this, but it's my only copy. Can you have it xeroxed and returned?"

I assured him that I could.

"Wonderful, wonderful. Can you see yourself out?"

As I walked back down the stairs, it struck me how remarkably uncurious my cousin had been about what kind of investigation I was conducting. I suppose, in his mind, there was only one thing to discover about the Latourette family: how tremendous we all were.

I never did get invited to see the estate.

. . .

The book was an anecdote-studded genealogy: *Latourette Annals in America*, "by Lyman E. Latourette, LL.B, M.A., LL.D," the title page proclaimed. Lyman E. had been a second-generation Oregon City resident. His father, Lyman D. C., was the one who had come to Oregon City in an oxcart, established one of the best farms in Clackamas County on the site of an Indian village and burying ground, set up the first bookstore on the West Coast, and married Lucy, Ezra Fisher's daughter. The author of the photo-copied book I now held in my hands was Ezra Fisher's grandson, Kenneth Scott Latourette's uncle, and my first cousin four times removed. He had written the book in 1954, when he was eighty-one years old.

Lyman E.'s methodology in compiling his annals seems to have been writing to all the cousins he could find, asking for their knowl-edge of family lore, and copying their responses into his book. One cousin had written back from Upstate New York, "I am a pretty busy woman just preparing for a week of rest and mental stimulus too, at Clifton Springs Sanitarium." It was a facility that, for one hundred years, offered treatment for wealthy patrons on the site of a sacred Onöndowa'ga hot springs in Upstate New York. Still, she'd managed to find time to include a fairly compre-hensive sketch of her branch of the family.

The book was written the year after my mother's birth, but she does not appear in its pages. My grandmother does, though, in a brief notation on page 97: "Patricia Ann, b. June 27, 1927, married Erich Lucas, b. Oct. 26, 1923." He'd gotten both of my grandparents' birth years wrong, but at least their names were spelled correctly.

When the writer recorded the entry for himself, he noted,

> Without being blessed with special mental or intellectual ability, he has, by applying himself through long hours and persistently following his objectives, won some measure of success. . . . Whatever success he has achieved will not be recounted for it is briefly stated in "Who is Who in Oregon, 1934–1936; 1942–1944," and "Who is Who on the Pacific Coast." He has been a firm believer in just laws, honestly administered and enforced; the American system of representative government as the best type thus far achieved in the process of evolution; the Christian religion as the best form of religion that the world has known, and the Golden Rule as the best precept to which individuals can cling.

Throughout the *Latourette Annals*, Lyman E. remained as steadfastly impressed with his ancestors as he was with himself. Overall, he believed his book had been able to "establish the important points" about the family:

> That they reached America with difficulty; that they escaped all perils; that they were industrious, honest, thrifty people; that they firmly believed in a type of Christian religion that was not dogmatic or intolerant of other beliefs; that they practiced the Golden Rule in daily life, and, as able, took an active part in building churches and upholding good government. They, like the great majority of peo-

ple in America have helped to make a better nation and a better world.

Unfortunately, all this emphasis on the Golden Rule didn't seem to make Lyman E. stop to consider whether his ancestors actually *had* treated other people as they would have liked to be treated themselves. He did not comment on the 1799 will that records a Latourette ancestor leaving "a Negro wench to his wife" and a "Negro named Jack" to his son. The only mention of Oregon's Indigenous people was an assurance that, by the time the Latourettes arrived, "the Indians were pushed back or absorbed into civilized ways." As with much writing about the effects of racism, his passive voice neatly elided the question of who did the pushing.

It was a letter from my own great-great-grandfather about breeding Jersey cows that prompted Lyman E. Latourette to reveal his true purpose for compiling the *Latourette Annals:*

> Sheldon's reference to genetics causes the writer to note that . . . ancient habits and customs will not much longer delay the application of scientific methods to human genetics, so that the continuous breeding of morons, kleptomaniacs, and other forms of debased life will be checked. . . . A few more generations may see the day when human genetics will be so applied as to greatly restrict the breeding of morons, etc., and also restrict excessive increase of population. Historical data about families will then be important.

As I scanned this paragraph, my eyes widened. *Historical data about families will then be important . . . so that the continuous breed-*

ing of morons, kleptomaniacs, and other forms of debased life will be checked? The *Latourette Annals* of Lyman E. Latourette wasn't just a nice scrapbook of family stories. It was a polemic—a justification for continuing Latourette existence in what its author foresaw to be an age of eugenics. And Lyman E. supposed that he had figured out who deserved to live and who deserved to die.

I loved my grandma Patty, and I love all my extended family, and I know that no one in my family today has inherited a desire to kill off the world's undesirable population. But still, as I paged through the photocopies I'd received from my Latourette cousin, I grieved.

I grieved the White supremacy I read between the lines there. Generation after generation of lounging about on chartreuse couches, insisting that our government is the best, our religion is the best, our family is literally more deserving of life than other people's families, and, oh, we got where we are today by our own hard work, and we treated everybody else exactly the way they wanted to be treated (pay no attention to the pushed-back Indians or the Negro wench). I grieved for everything spoken on the pages of my family's lore and for everything that had gone unspoken.

I grieved, too, the way I saw myself reflected in that book's pages. The White supremacy I knew lived in my own heart. And the way that I, too, prefer to speak about my own accomplishments and remain silent about my sins.

How do we measure the sound of silence? How can we ever know what has or has not resulted from a word not spoken?

In 1864, thirteen years after Jacob Vanderpool's exile from Oregon and seven years after exclusion was enshrined in the state constitution, a Democratic state legislator proposed an amendment to the Oregon Constitution. George Lawson wanted the state's founding document to read "that a negro, Chinaman or Indian has no right that a white man is bound to respect, and that a white man may murder, rob, rape, shoot, stab and cut any of these worthless and vagabond races, without being called to account." Lawson proposed that these acts of breathtaking violence should actually be considered "acts of bravery and chivalry." The only limitation he wanted to place upon his catalog of heinous deeds was that they should not be undertaken in times and places when other White people might be "troubled" by seeing them carried out. Essentially, Lawson wanted the right to lynch preserved in the Oregon State Constitution.

Lawson's fellow legislators were stunned into silence. They tabled the motion and ultimately did not vote it into law, but neither did they censure Lawson or run him out of their assembly.

Still, their silence did not erase his sentiment.

I wonder, can we draw a straight line between the 1864 Oregon legislators' silence in the face of such a horrific proposal and the lynching of Alonzo Tucker in Coos Bay, Oregon, in 1902? Between those legislators' silence and the murder of Ethiopian student Mulugeta Seraw by three White supremacists in downtown Portland in 1988? Between the silence in 1864 and the race-based murders of Ricky John Best and Taliesin Myrddin Namkai-Meche by a self-avowed White supremacist on a Portland light-rail train in 2017?

Or were those murders, and the hate that fueled them, enabled by the silence of the millions of other White Oregonians who came in between?

When my son Josiah was ten, he fell off a scooter and gashed his shin. My mom stuck a large adhesive bandage over the wound, and we soon forgot all about it.

But a month or so later, we had all gathered in the living room to watch TV, when my husband wrinkled up his nose. "What's that smell?"

We finally traced the offending odor to its source: our son's leg. Josiah rolled up his pants, and there was the bandage Nana had given him a month before. It had never occurred to him to take it off. It was winter, and since he'd been wearing pants and was too old for help in the bath, none of us had any idea the bandage was still there. When we peeled it off, the source of the stench was clear: The wound had become pussy, green, and gangrenous.

"It's a good thing you didn't wait any longer on this one," our pediatrician said the next morning. We embarked on a regimen of antibiotics and cleansing treatments. To this day, Josiah's shin bears a deeply cratered scar.

Staying silent about White supremacy is like putting a bandage on a deep wound: Maybe, for a while, you can forget about it.

But sooner or later, it stinks.

Osheta Moore wrote in *Dear White Peacemakers* about the hate crime that first rocked her world. She was seventeen years old the summer James Byrd, Jr., was dragged behind a pickup truck for three miles and killed (a crime eerily similar to the murder recalled by Carl Boone, the formerly enslaved Kentuckian who'd witnessed his enslaver tie a man to a horse and drag him through a field until he died). When Osheta went to church the Sunday after Byrd's death, in her hometown just two and a half hours from the site of the murder, she was crushed by her White pastor's silence. "He didn't say a single thing," Moore wrote. "No one said anything. . . . There were no witnesses to my pain and the systemic violence that caused it."

That was the moment when Osheta, "because of the church's silence on race and racism, . . . built a wall" in her heart against White people. "I spent the next fourteen years," she said, "cautious of every single White person, waiting for them to harm me with their willful ignorance."

Our silence hurts our friends.

Why does the church, in particular, so often choose the way of silence? From Ezra Fisher and his congregation to the clergy whom Martin Luther King, Jr., addressed from his Birmingham jail cell to the pastor and fellow church members of a hurting seventeen-year-old girl desperate for a witness to her pain, why is it *church* that sometimes seems so uniquely unable to respond with human emotion to the suffering around us? Are we afraid, perhaps, that speaking out about injustice will expose our own hypocrisy?

Church, of all places, is supposed to be based on the simple premise that grace comes to us all because we all have fallen short. Some denominations even build a practice of verbal confession of sin right into the fabric of their weekly services. But somehow, for many of us, the place that is supposed to provide the most freedom to be honest about our shortcomings ends up being the place where we are least likely to let any piece of our humanity slip through. Instead of letting all our grief and shame hang out, in church we may be even more likely to button it up and paste a smile on top.

I wonder if we in the church have forgotten who we are.

We are the church—the gathered community of those who believe that the immortal, invisible God, who wraps himself in light as with a garment, spoke but a word and sent all the atoms of the universe tumbling into that miracle we call *being*.

We are the church—the gathered community of those who believe that this impossibly vast, unendingly great God took on human flesh: the whisper of a seed planted in the womb of an unmarried girl named Mary, which grew into a baby who was laid to sleep in a feeding trough and welcomed by a ragtag group of night-shift shepherds and foreign astrologers.

We are the church—the gathered community of those who believe that that baby grew into a God-man named Jesus, who walked among us to reveal the beat of his Father's heart: touching the ones who had been deemed untouchable, speaking to the ones who were thought unspeakable, reaching out with a love that was fierce and gentle, patient and insistent, all-forgiving and all-demanding. Jesus asked the rich young man to impoverish himself for the good of his neighbors and praised the poor old woman for giving all she had. He saved an adulterous woman from execution and publicly invited himself to the home of a corrupt tax official with whom no one else wanted to be seen. Rich ones, poor ones, old ones, young ones, powerful ones, weak ones, healthy ones, disabled ones, self-righteous ones, shame-filled ones, soldiers of the occupying empire and panhandlers in the street—Jesus came for them all.

We are the church—the gathered community of those who believe that in the fullness of time, this Jesus bled out every drop of his love for humanity on the cross, taking the death that belonged to us all and turning it upside down into the promise of abundant and never-ending life.

We are the church—the gathered community of those who believe that no matter where we have come from or what we have been, the living Jesus sees clear through to the very marrow of our souls, extends his scarred hands to us, and calls us *Beloved*.

If we could remember all that, I don't think we'd waste another minute trying to pretend we're something that we're not.

I don't think we'd waste another minute on silence.

I soon learned that the opposite of silence is not just any kind of speech. As I got to know Jacob Vanderpool, I found myself wanting to get better at speaking out about racism. I attempted to speak out about racial justice in my classroom and in my community. Sometimes, I felt I was simply making a hash of things. Other times, I was able to see some kind of positive shift as a result of my speech. But the first time I spoke out, I seemed to mostly just make people angry.

In the summer of 2020, I preached a sermon pleading with my fellow church members to listen to the stories people of color were sharing with us. Some thanked me for my words. But others were incensed. I didn't think I had said anything particularly radical, but the criticisms found me, all the same. This was the summer of Covid-19 lockdowns and protests over the death of George Floyd. Our mostly White, working-class, politically mixed church sat on the edge of a politically mixed county that bordered decidedly liberal Portland. Downtown, clashes between protestors and police had been escalating all summer. Everyone was on edge. So I should not have been surprised when the responses came in: an outraged comment on the church website; a vehement remark in an unrelated all-church survey; a quick jab at my husband, who is the pastor of our church. *Churches shouldn't be political!* seemed to be the general message of dissent.

I shouldn't have been surprised, but I was disappointed. I had wanted to say something helpful, something my church would hear. I wondered why churches could be "political" about topics like abortion or prayer in schools, but not race. I wondered if there was anything I could have said differently to help them think again.

So I reached out to each person who had lodged a complaint. I told each one that I wanted to understand where they were coming from. Each agreed to meet me for a socially distanced conversation, on a walk through a field near our church or on the outdoor patio of a nearby restaurant. I tried to walk the line between not apologizing for what I'd said and not enraging them all over again. I tried to listen.

I'd been reading *Divided by Faith*, Michael O. Emerson and Christian Smith's sociological exploration of White evangelical feelings about race. It struck me, as I listened to my congregation members' thoughts, that their sentiments were the same as the ones elucidated in that book, even though the book had been written more than twenty years earlier. Two decades had passed, and White Christians were still making the same kinds of arguments: *Racial reconciliation should be about individual acts of kindness, not policy changes. The most Christian approach to the whole situation is "colorblindness." God helps those who help themselves.*

Most puzzling to me was the argument that racism doesn't actually exist. "Not since Martin Luther King, Jr., showed us the way," one person explained. "He took care of it, and now it's gone." A couple of people suggested that even if racism did exist, it shouldn't be such a big deal. "My parents had a difficult life, but they worked hard and overcame their obstacles. Why can't Black people?" was a common theme.

Even though I'd set out to listen, I felt that I needed, in my own not-particularly-well-informed way, to try to speak again. After all, I'd also been listening to my brothers and sisters of color that summer—reading their op-eds, following their Twitter feeds, having one-on-one conversations—and I knew that for these friends, racism was most definitely not gone from America. All they wanted was to be able to peacefully *live*—to go for a run in their own neighborhood, to stand in the middle of their own apartment, to buy a bag of Skittles—without feeling as though they might at any moment be hunted down and killed. How could I convince my fellow church members to hear those pleas?

With one person, I tried sharing statistics I'd recently gleaned from a YouTube video made by Phil Vischer, the creator of the evangelical children's show *VeggieTales*. How disparities in the disbursement of the G.I. Bill, for example, had led to vast inequities in home ownership for Black versus White families, which in turn had led to extreme differences in net wealth. But my conversation partner wasn't having it.

"Numbers!" they bristled. "Don't talk to me about numbers! I know how easy it is to manipulate statistics!"

In another conversation, I took a different tack. I shared some stories about racism I'd heard from my friend Gerald Baugh, whose story, I thought, was the modern-day Jacob Vanderpool's. Gerald had moved out of the Oregon area—after spending part of his career in hotel development, no less—because the racism and inhospitality of the Portland-area business community was so relentless. But those stories were met with the same resentment. "Anecdotes," my friend responded. "You're just giving me anecdotes. That doesn't prove anything."

I was at a loss. If I couldn't use numbers and I couldn't use anecdotes, what was left?

So I did the only other thing I knew how to do. In each of these meetings, there came a moment when I ended up leveling with my conversation partner. "I know racism is real," I told them, "because it's in me."

Each time I made that statement, I observed a subtle shift in the person's demeanor: a slight relaxing of body language, a small catch of breath, a gentle softening of the face. No longer was I an adversary with superior knowledge, trying to prove that I possessed all wisdom, and they were backward and bigoted. For an instant, there was a glimmer of *Oh, we're going to get real.* Vulnerability, rather than proof, was the more salient currency. The most effective opposite of silence was not mere speech; it was self-disclosure.

It lasted only an instant. Then the sparring gloves were raised again.

"Well, they probably feel the same way about you," one replied.

"I question the meaning of that word," another responded.

But still. In those moments, I glimpsed a way forward. It wouldn't be forged by proving the skeptics wrong; it would be found in exposing the soft underbelly of my own shame.

Perhaps, for those of us who desire to act justly and love mercy, this is the way: to walk forward in our own humility. Sometimes the most powerful answer to "Racism doesn't exist anymore"—especially for those of us who are White—is "Yes, it does. It's right here."

We must be careful how we do this, of course. We can't just publicly confess in order to receive absolution. We can't carry our shame from one individual Black person to another, begging for forgiveness. We can only stand confident in the knowledge that, in Christ, we are already forgiven. In the knowledge that forgiveness itself is what makes it possible for us to speak up and take action. "Forgiveness does not contradict the pursuit of justice," said pastor Tim Keller. "It is its precondition."

And we can't confess to make ourselves seem better than those who haven't recognized their need to confess yet. The reality of the White supremacy that lies curled inside us is never a source of arrogance, never a cudgel. It can be only a genuine lament. Lament that this evil found a way to hook us and we didn't even know it.

Lament that we somehow welcomed it in and don't know how to get it out again.

There are support groups for alcoholics and addicts and those who struggle with mental illness and every other type of stigmatized shame. What if there were a space where White people could examine the legacy our society has spent hundreds of years pouring into our laps? What if there were a place where I could go to say, "My name is Sarah, and I don't want to be a White supremacist any longer"?

What if there were a place where we could be loved enough to be totally honest about all our sins, whatever they might be?

What if that place were the church?

Chapter Nine

The Exile

Jacob Vanderpool's newspaper advertisement, 1851.
From the *Oregon Statesman*.

One week after the verdict was handed down, Jacob Vanderpool ran his ad in the *Statesman* again. With less than a month of Oregon residence remaining, he was apparently determined to make a go of his business for as long as legally possible. Or perhaps he was hoping for some last-minute reversal that never came.

In that same edition of the paper, just a few pages over from Vanderpool's ad, a brief article appeared. In its entirety, this is how it read:

THE BLACK LAW

The law prohibiting negroes and mulattoes from coming into and residing in Oregon, was decided to be constitutional and valid, by Chief Justice Nelson, in a case brought before him last week. The defendant (colored) was directed to leave the Territory within thirty days from the date of the decree. This we suppose is but the re-affirmation of a well settled doctrine—one which would be sanctioned by the whole Court. At least, we understand one of the other Judges fully endorses the opinion rendered.

But the re-affirmation of a well settled doctrine. This article, affirming Oregon's "well settled doctrine" of Black exclusion, was reprinted in newspapers as far away as Woodville, Mississippi. Would-be pioneers all over the country had been put on notice: If they were Black, they would not be welcome in the Oregon Territory.

In his own newspaper, abolitionist Frederick Douglass published a different article about Oregon's exclusion law:

> Even in the so-called free territory of Oregon, the colored American citizen, though he may possess all the qualities and qualifications which make a man a good citizen, is driven out like a beast in the forest, made to sacrifice every interest dear to him, and forbidden the privilege to take the portion of the soil which the government says that every citizen shall enjoy.

For three weeks after his trial, Vanderpool continued to run his ad in the paper. But on the fourth week, with the thirty-day dead-

line for his "removal" looming, the *Statesman* finally stopped carrying the little advertisement with the picture of the bird in the
grass. Like a beast in the forest, Jacob Vanderpool had been driven
out.

John McLoughlin founded the town and presided over it as mayor.
Theophilus Magruder pressed the charges. Thomas Nelson decided the case. Ezra Fisher, and hundreds like him, read about it in
the papers and did nothing. All four played a role, whether directly
or indirectly, in the expulsion of Jacob Vanderpool from the state
of Oregon—and by extension, in the expulsion of Eliza, Jane,
Amelia, and Martin, who would never be summoned to join their
husband and father in Oregon City.

When my great-great-grandfather's brother came to Oregon in
1848, he built what would become an empire: the houses on the
hill, the park bearing the family name, all the generations of Latourette cousins who marched up and down Oregon's history books.
If Jacob Vanderpool had been allowed to stay—if his children had
been welcomed with as much hospitality and grace as my family's
children—how might the Vanderpools, too, have shaped this state
I call home?

McLoughlin, Magruder, Nelson, and Fisher played a role, as
well, in the expulsion of the untold thousands of men, women, and
children who would not come after. Exclusion laws remained on
the books in Oregon until 1926. By the 1920s, Oregon was home to
the largest Ku Klux Klan chapter west of the Mississippi River. By
2016, *The Atlantic* called Portland, Oregon, "the Whitest city in
America." In 2020, the FBI ranked Oregon as the state with the

twelfth highest number of hate crimes, the third-most per capita. In 2022, more than 686,000 Oregonians voted to retain language permitting slavery as a punishment for a crime in the state's constitution. As I have been writing this book, the Proud Boys have been demonstrating every Friday afternoon on McLoughlin Boulevard, less than a mile from my house.

This is the place that McLoughlin, Magruder, Nelson, and Fisher made. It is the place that all of us in Oregon—by our actions and our inactions—are still making.

All four of those early pioneers have been thoroughly documented and highly extolled. Their homes have been added to the National Register of Historic Places. Their correspondence has been published. Their biographies have been written. Their names have been painted on the walls in the Oregon State Capitol.

This is not to say that everything they did was a sham or that we should begin to universally revile those whom we have universally praised. This is simply a call to think again. Think bigger. Look at the whole picture of what has been done—and what has been left undone. Think differently about whom we have remembered and whom we have forgotten.

As for Jacob Vanderpool, the man who simply wanted to provide persons from the country with meals at regular hours, he seemed to vanish without a trace.

On a foggy and frosted morning the week before Christmas, I drove to Salem to see the Capitol. I wanted to see their names: *McLoughlin, Nelson, Fisher*. I wanted to see how the men who made this place had been memorialized.

A crash on the interstate diverted me to McLoughlin Boulevard, the two-lane highway that winds along the Willamette River. Wraiths of fog twisted above the sullen brown surface of the water. In Oregon City, rusted hulks of abandoned factories sat hunched around Willamette Falls, blocking the view. The farmlands were acres of muddy puddles. In places, the fog lay so low in the cold that the distant tips of evergreen trees seemed to poke above the clouds. Sometimes the fog would thin enough to allow light to slant in through the hazelnut groves or to illumine the empty gallows where trails of last year's hop vines still hung. Around the town of Donald, the road wound into a patch of fog so dense I almost forgot I was still alive. Gone were the trees, the fields, the roadside farmhouses. There was only me, and gray, and the occasional blink of oncoming traffic—headlights that would pop up about ten feet away, glide past, and leave me alone again in a world that had ceased to exist.

Finally, as I wound through the streets of Salem, I saw the smooth white marble of the Oregon Capitol rising from the mist.

"Everything you see here is through the lens of 1938," my tour guide explained. It was one of only five Art Deco Capitol buildings in the entire country, I later learned. The tour guide herself was quintessential Oregon: a padded red-plaid flannel shirt, Birkenstocks with socks, multiple ear piercings. She was about fifty years old, with frizzy salt-and-pepper hair and pink cheeks that peeked above her black cotton face mask. There was no one else there for a tour, so I got her undivided attention.

Mabel walked me around the rotunda, which depicted Oregon's history through a series of four murals—a *1938* version of Oregon's history, she was careful to emphasize. In the first mural, Captain Robert Gray and his immaculately laundered crew were shown landing at the mouth of the Columbia River, receiving gifts from the Indigenous people gathered there. "I tell the kids it's like if you went over to a neighbor's house that you'd never met, 'discovered' their dog, and named it something else," Mabel said.

"That's a good analogy," I replied.

"The next one's my favorite," she went on, after we'd stared at Captain Gray for a while. We turned to gaze at the Lewis and Clark party. "This is Celilo Falls, where there was still an important Native fishing site when this mural was painted. It hadn't been dammed yet. See Sacajawea there? And there's York, who was enslaved by Clark."

"Was he the first African American to come to Oregon?" I asked.

"I think there was someone else first, maybe in Astoria?" Mabel replied.

I nodded and explained, "I'm interested in the African American presence here."

"Well, I'm not supposed to say this," Mabel said, "but we were crap at that." Her pink cheeks flushed even pinker above her mask, perhaps because she realized she'd said something she wasn't supposed to say.

I looked at York for a while. Everyone else in the picture was holding something: a gun, a staff, an oar, a canoe. Some of the figures were talking to each other, some gazing expectantly at the river, some launching a boat into the water. York was the only person in the entire mural with no tool in his hands. The White men in the party were busy extending an empire, while the horseback American Indians looked on from a distance, holding their reins. But the artist had chosen to depict York as idle, sitting hunched on a rock, staring at the ground, hands empty. Whatever talents, resources, and hard work York had undoubtedly brought to the group were not shown here.

"I can't even read this next caption out loud," Mabel said as we turned to the third corner of the room. "I hate it." *The first white women to cross the continent welcomed by Dr. McLoughlin at Fort Vancouver, 1836,* it read. I wondered if it was the word *white* that Mabel choked on. "But it was important, I guess," she went on, "because after these supposedly soft, helpless women made it across the continent . . ."

". . . it opened the way for the rest of the Oregon Trail," I finished, and we turned, after a moment, to the final corner of the room, where the men, women, children, dogs, and covered wagons of the Oregon Trail filled the scene.

"Now, this one we changed our language on because of the pandemic," Mabel explained. "But—how are we saying it now?—this was the largest overland migration in history not due to war or something." She seemed a bit confused about what the new language was supposed to be. But she hit her stride as she continued. "One year, nine hundred people came across the Oregon Trail, and over six hundred of them were under the age of sixteen, and the wagons were full of their belongings, so they walked the whole way. Fifteen or twenty miles a day, without full calories either.

And they saved their shoes for the mountains and snow, so they basically walked across the entire continent barefoot." For all her embarrassment over Oregon's treatment of African Americans and its reception of the first White women, Mabel was clearly proud of the Oregon Trail pioneers.

"Why did you change the language because of the pandemic?" I asked.

"Well, because of Black Lives Matter, you know," she said. "People were coming on our virtual web tours and asking, 'When did they start killing people?' Well, nobody was killing people." After a beat, she added, "At least, most people weren't."

Then Mabel took me into the House and Senate chambers, which were lined with the names of the 158 people judged in 1938 to have best contributed to the founding of Oregon. There was Thomas Nelson, the judge who'd forced Jacob Vanderpool to leave the Territory. John McLoughlin, the "Father of Oregon," who'd been mayor of Oregon City the summer of Vanderpool's trial. Ezra Fisher, the pastor and professor who'd neglected to come to Vanderpool's defense.

There were other names I recognized. Peter Burnett, who'd argued for the implementation of the very first exclusion law. Three names from an 1857 Constitutional Convention debate about how to word the law restricting voting rights to White citizens only: Matthew Deady, who'd proposed that only White people should be allowed to vote in Oregon; Thomas Dryer, who'd wanted a "standard" set up to settle who was White; and Delazon Smith, who'd hesitated to insert the word *free* or *pure* before *white* because it would make the law more difficult to execute. Their names encircled the state's legislative chambers.

There were some American Indian names in the lists: Marie Aioe Dorion, the Iowa Tribe wife of a French-Sioux fur trapper, lauded because, owing to the European ancestry of one of her children's four grandparents, she "gave birth to the first child born in the Oregon Country in whose genes the white race was represented." And a few others: Sacajawea, Chief Concomly, Chief Joseph.

But there was also General Howard, who "led the charge against Chief Joseph"; James W. Nesmith, an "Indian fighter"; and Philip H. Sheridan, who "helped disperse the Indians." I wondered how Chief Joseph would have felt, to be hailed as a hero on the same wall as the man who had hunted him down. He had spent months keeping his band of seven hundred Nez Perce men, women, and children safe from General Howard's two thousand soldiers on a 1,100-mile journey through the mountains in an attempt to reach Canada. They had fought hard and fled hard. Two hundred of their people died along the way. Ultimately, they were captured and sent to reservations. Chief Joseph never returned to his beloved homeland, but a marker in the town of Joseph, Oregon, memorializes his birthplace. And in 1938, some committee of Oregonians had decided that both Chief Joseph and General Howard ought to be remembered as people important to the "development of Oregon."

"Who's on the top of the building?" I asked Mabel, thinking of the large golden statue I'd seen atop the rotunda as I got out of my car.

"Oh, that's Every Man," she explained. "With an ax in his hand, representing hard work, and a tarp, representing shelter. It's everyone who ever came to Oregon."

. . .

It was a tomb, I realized as I drove away. A large white sarcopha-gus memorializing the death of one age of this land and celebrating the rise of another. It was a monument to White supremacy.

The murals told the story: White people came here, and the American Indians welcomed us in. White people explored here, and the American Indians looked on benevolently. White people brought their women here, and the American Indians were gone. White people moved in and settled and filled the land as far as the eye could see.

There were no Black names, that I could discover, in the House or Senate chambers. The legislators who'd determined, back in 1844, to exclude Black lives from the state of Oregon had evi-dently succeeded. The only person of African descent remem-bered in the entire Capitol was the apparently hapless York, sitting idly in the corner of the mural while his enslaver explored the con-tinent that his countrymen believed was their Manifest Destiny to control.

It was a 1938 view of Oregon history, as Mabel had said. But she "wasn't supposed to say" that Oregon's history of interacting with Black people was "crap." Someone, in the year 2020, had at-tempted to revamp the language about the Oregon Trail mural but had also instructed the tour guides to keep silent about Oregon's history of exclusion.

Oregon's Capitol may be a striking example of White suprem-acy, but it's hardly alone. Only a handful of states in the entire country have ever elected a Black governor.

Should we scrub the murals, expunge the names, topple the statues?

Or should we begin telling a new kind of story—a truer kind of story—about what has happened here?

On my trip home, the interstate was clear and the fog had lifted. As I drove, I kept my eyes on the mountains at the far edge of the Willamette Valley. They were dusted with new-fallen snow.

On Juneteenth, my friend Nancy attended a celebration in Oregon City. At the festival, she saw a sign bearing a few sentences about Jacob Vanderpool, snapped a picture, and texted it to me: "Here's your guy."

On the bottom of the sign was the name of an organization: Oregon Black Pioneers. I hadn't known such a group existed. According to their website, Oregon Black Pioneers provided consultations, exhibitions, educational programming, and events, all designed to commemorate the state's earliest Black residents. I emailed right away.

I felt sheepish disclosing my identity as a White writer working on the story of Jacob Vanderpool. Would they think I was sticking my oar in where I didn't belong? But when executive director Zachary Stocks wrote back, he was nothing but kind. He responded to several of my email queries in a row, and eventually he shared a whole electronic file with me. "Here is most of what we have on Jacob Vanderpool in terms of primary sources," he wrote. "Hopefully this will be of use to you!"

And there, in a shared Google Drive folder filled with clippings, Oregon Black Pioneers taught me more about the life of Jacob Vanderpool in the span of a few minutes than I'd managed to find in years on my own.

There was the 1850 census, with the family members I hadn't known existed until that very moment: Eliza, Jane, Amelia, and Martin. There was the 1870 census, which recorded that at age fifty, Jacob Vanderpool had lived in San Francisco and worked as a "packer of hardware." In 1870, there was no mention of the children, who would have been twenty and twenty-three, but there was a new wife, Mary, age forty-nine. And there was the 1880 census, which had Jacob and Mary still living in San Francisco. Now a sixty-year-old man, Jacob worked as a school janitor.

In the online archives of the *San Francisco Examiner*, I found a school board report: "The Committee on Janitors reported in favor of the following appointments to fill places lately declared vacant." Buried in a long list of schools and names (the lobby where aspiring new janitors gathered had apparently been "literally packed with first-class janitorial material") was "Jackson-street, Jacob Vanderpool." But I couldn't find Jackson Street School in San Francisco mentioned anywhere else online. Evidently, the hallways Jacob Vanderpool had spent his twilight years polishing were gone.

Zachary emailed me later with another newspaper clipping. This one listed Jacob Vanderpool as a shareholder in the Young Men's Union Beneficial Society. Zachary wasn't sure what that was. After an hour or two of digging, I emailed him back to share an article I'd found listing the Young Men's Union Beneficial Society as one of several Black activist groups that had paraded in San Francisco following the ratification of the Fifteenth Amendment, guaranteeing Black men the right to vote.

I loved imagining Jacob Vanderpool the activist, marching in a parade. How precious it would have felt to Vanderpool, after being legally expelled from one state, to march in a neighboring state, decades later, in celebration of the long-awaited right to vote.

The last item in the Oregon Black Pioneers folder was an 1886 voter registration list. On October 16, 1886, a sixty-six-year-old Jacob Vanderpool had registered to vote in San Francisco County. It would be his final recorded act. I later found an 1887 record listing Mary Vanderpool as a widow.

But I kept wondering about Eliza, Amelia, Jane, and Martin. Had Jacob traveled directly from Oregon City to San Francisco and married someone else? Had he never returned to his wife and children in New York? There were many years between 1851 and 1870, of course, and a Civil War to boot. He might have gone back, and Eliza might have died, and the children might have grown and launched, all before Vanderpool married Mary and made his way west again. There was no reason to suppose that he'd simply abandoned his family. But the gap bothered me.

I searched online databases over and over, typing in various combinations of all the data points I knew: Jacob, Vanderpool, 1820, Black, West Indies, Oregon, San Francisco, New York.

There's no good way to capture any sort of suspense and drama in this search. I just kept hitting the Enter button again, and again, and again. Finally, I got lucky: a tax record from the state of New York, 1865. Two people paid a carriage tax that year—essentially, a tax on operating a horse-drawn taxicab. Jacob Vanderpool and Martin Vanderpool.

Those two little names, scrawled on a ledger more than 150 years before, opened up a whole new chapter in my understanding of Jacob Vanderpool's life. He *had* returned to New York, it seemed, in between Oregon and California. I couldn't find what had happened to Eliza, Amelia, or Jane, but here was Martin: fifteen years old and driving a New York City taxicab with his father.

Even as I grieved the insensible pressures this family had faced, I rejoiced that Jacob Vanderpool had made it home.

The Oregon Black Pioneers file also suggested an answer to one final mystery. Jacob Vanderpool had announced in his newspaper ad that his boarding house was located across the street from the *Statesman* offices—but where was that? I'd asked the Clackamas County Historical Society, and they'd searched their files and come up empty. I'd riffled through microfiche at the County Records office and found nothing. I'd come across an online source that referred to the *Statesman* building as the "Friers Building," but no one seemed to know where that had stood either. It turned out that an Oregon Black Pioneers volunteer had managed to find an answer, and the file contained a picture of their map. A student working with Ross Sutherland of the Bush House Museum in Salem had circled one particular building and labeled it "Jacob Vanderpool" with a brown pen.

The south side of Main Street, between Third and Fourth Streets. Just down from the Methodist Church. The Oregon Black Pioneers folder also contained a reference on the front page of the very first *Statesman* confirming this location: The new paper wanted its patrons to know that its offices were located "first north of the M. E. Church." Jacob Vanderpool had operated his business opposite the *Statesman* office, and the *Statesman* office was north of the M. E. Church, and the church had been located on the corner of Third and Main. Right there in the Oregon Black Pioneers files, in brown pen.

The Methodist Church had been etched into one of the very first pictures of Oregon City I had examined, the one on the cover of *Holden's Dollar Magazine*. When I looked at it again, I wondered if Vanderpool's Oregon Saloon and Boarding House had been the tiny little building just to the left of the church in the picture. Or perhaps Jacob Vanderpool had built a new structure, just there in the gap next to the church, right below the fault line between the two cliffs. Perhaps the place had been right there in front of my eyes all along.

Then I saw another painting in the file: "Oregon City on the Willamette River," by John Mix Stanley. Sometime between 1850 and 1852, Stanley had stood on the hill overlooking Oregon City and painted its downtown buildings, larger and more easily identifiable than in the etching. I found the Methodist Church spire in the painting easily enough. Kitty-corner across the street from the church was a white two-story building that must have been the location of the *Statesman* office. And back on the same side of Main Street as the church, just opposite the *Statesman* office, was a dark-gray two-story building on the corner of a grassy lot. There it was, painted in color, in the same year Jacob Vanderpool had lived in it: the Oregon Saloon and Boarding House. The artist had also painted a distraught-looking Indian couple in the corner of his work, on their way out of town.

I went for a walk. I started at the spot near Thirteenth and Main where I knew Ezra Fisher had lived and worked, the site of the original Oregon City Baptist Church and Oregon City College. I walked past the courthouse that had long since replaced the wooden one where Jacob Vanderpool was held. Past the site where Theophilus Magruder had operated the hotel where Thomas Nelson stayed. I got as close as I could to Third and Fourth Streets. It took me seven minutes, strolling at a leisurely pace, to get from one end of Main Street—where all these men and their plans had closed in on Jacob Vanderpool—to the other.

But I could not approach the exact spot where Jacob Vanderpool had lived and worked. A fence now surrounded the old industrial area near the falls, the site where John McLoughlin's original mill had bloated and spawned acres of later factories, now derelict and abandoned. Somewhere in there, amid the hulking concrete walls and broken windows, was the very place where Jacob Vanderpool had tried, for a few brief months in the summer of 1851, to welcome guests to Oregon.

The fence was up because these blocks would soon become an active construction site. In 2019, the Confederated Tribes of the Grand Ronde—the descendants of the Clackamas people and other tribes sent to the Grand Ronde reservation in the year that Oregon became a state—purchased the twenty-three-acre property. They plan to revitalize the site with environmental restoration, native plants, and mixed-use development that will provide visitors with access to the falls and to the stories of their people. The primary goal of the Confederated Tribes, in retaking stewardship of the site, is to "heal the land."

The descendants of the Clowwewalla, long banished from their ancestral homeland near the falls of the Willamette, are returning to Charcowah once again.

Chapter Ten

From Exclusion to Community

"Sometimes I wonder," said Thomas.

"Wonder what?"

"If one of them will ever say, Gee, those damn Indians might have had an idea or two. Shouldn't have got rid of them all. Maybe we missed out."

Louis laughed. Thomas laughed. They laughed together at the idea.

—Louise Erdrich, *The Night Watchman*

Rare is the ministry praying that they would be worthy of the giftedness of Black minds and hearts.

—Austin Channing Brown, *I'm Still Here*

Your name is not racist, it's Beloved.

—Osheta Moore, *Dear White Peacemakers*

Oregon City is changing. Some things remain just as they were after Jacob Vanderpool's expulsion in 1851—there are still no Black-owned businesses in the downtown core. But some things are wildly new. The descendants of the Clowwewalla have returned to steward the falls once again. The factories will be coming down; the traditional salmon fishing has resumed. And in 2022, after recalling an outspokenly racist mayor, the people of Oregon City elected their first-ever mayor of color. "This community is in a period of transition," Denyse McGriff responded when asked about her historic election as the city's first Black mayor. "We have a great deal of diversity in Oregon City. . . . It's just all part of the bigger picture."

But it was a bigger picture that I was still not sure how I fit into. Most of the work I had done so far—finding Jacob Vanderpool and wrestling with the implications of his story in my own life—I had at least been able to *begin* by myself. Turning from ignorance to empathy, I could begin to do alone at the public library. Turning from clenched fists to open hands, I could begin to do alone with my checkbook. Turning from supremacy to shalom, I could begin to do in my own prayer journal. Even turning from silence to self-disclosure, I could begin to do in my own mostly White community. But if I wanted to turn fully from the legacy of exclusion, I would have to find a way to connect with others.

Just as I could not have found out what had happened to Jacob Vanderpool without the help of the Oregon Black Pioneers, I could not sit alone at my desk and manufacture the beloved community.

"White people are the most segregated people in America," wrote Heather McGhee. Seventy-five percent of White Americans report that their social networks are "entirely white." As a daughter of Oregon, living in a mostly White suburb of the Whitest city in America, attending a mostly White church and sending my children to mostly White schools, I grieved that this was mostly true of me as well.

And I did not know what to do about it.

Almost twenty years before I'd ever heard of Jacob Vanderpool, in September 1999, I stood alone on a hill in Livingstonia, Malawi. More specifically, I stood alone near a capital *E* on a hill in Livingstonia. Forty years before my visit, many hands had dragged large stones across that open knoll, arranging them to spell out the letters and numbers that still stretched through the grass: E P H E S I A N S 2:1 4.

The story—as my host had told me that morning while driving me up the winding road, before she dropped me off at the top of the mountain—dated back to 1959. In that year, there had been no road. When conflict broke out in the lower-lying regions between British colonists and Malawians fighting for independence, the little mission on the hill had been reachable only by foot or by air. The mission agency had had no way to contact the British staff of Livingstonia's hospital, church, and school, so they'd sent a small plane to drop a message, indicating the date and time they would come back to evacuate.

But when the airplane returned, there were no waiting missionaries. No one had packed their bags; no one was eager to escape to safety. Instead, the pilots peered down from their cockpit at the letters on the hill. I suppose, being missionary pilots, they traveled with Bibles, or perhaps they'd hidden all the words of Ephesians in their hearts, ready for instant recall. Somehow, anyway, they'd deciphered the message. Ephesians 2:14—*For he himself is our peace, who has made the two groups one and has destroyed the barrier, the dividing wall of hostility.*

The verse in its original context refers to the way the love of Jesus erased division between first-century Gentiles and first-century Jews. Its meaning on the hill in Livingstonia was just as clear: There was no fear of violence between Black and White in that place. Peace had replaced hostility. The missionaries would not be beating hasty retreats. They left the rocks to stand as a testament to the peace of Christ. Forty years later, a warm breeze riffled my hair as I walked among the stones and marveled.

Back then, at age twenty, I was awed both by the artifact from an earlier time and by the sentiment it spoke to. It was clearly significant—*this was a place where the power of Jesus defeated the powers of war!*—but it also didn't seem entirely real or relevant to my own life. To a White American college student in the late 1990s, interracial conflict seemed remote and foreign. The forty years that stood between the rejection of colonialism in Malawi and the day I walked on that hilltop seemed much longer to me at age twenty than it does now.* Today, I marvel not at the *length* of the gap between my visit and those stones' original planting but at its brevity.

As I grew into adulthood back in the United States and gradually gained an awareness of the immediacy of racial conflict in my

---

*Truly, the span was but a blink in the country's history. Dr. Hastings Kamuzu Banda, who became Malawi's prime minister in the aftermath of the violence that did not reach Livingstonia, did not step down until 1994, just five years before I visited. I got to witness the country's second-ever democratic election when I was there in 1999.

own country—the Ferguson riots, the Charleston shooting, my growing sense of my own implicit racism—I often reflected on the message on the hill in Livingstonia. But now it was the hilltop that seemed remote and foreign. Somewhere, sometime, some people had experienced enough of the presence of Christ that they had chosen to remain among people whom they might otherwise have feared. But how exactly did that help the shouting crowds and police in riot gear that I saw on my social media feed or on the evening news? How was Jesus going to destroy the dividing wall of hostility *here*?

I began to think, too, about the complicating forces of colonialism in the story of the Livingstonian missionaries. They had felt safe enough to stay—but weren't they still colonizers? It was nice that the Malawians there had not chosen violence, but if everyone in Malawi had operated that way, would the country still be under British rule? Jesus may have destroyed the barrier wall of hostility between people of different races in Livingstonia, but he had also inspired the civil disobedience of activists like Martin Luther King, Jr., and countless others. "I would not hesitate to say," King wrote from his Birmingham jail, just four years after the stones in Livingstonia were placed, "that it is unfortunate that so-called demonstrations are taking place in Birmingham at this time, but I would say in more emphatic terms that it is even more unfortunate that the white power structure of this city left the Negro community with no other alternative."

At twenty, I wanted my imagined picture of missionaries and Malawians arranging letters and numbers on the hill to be a triumphant capstone to my reflections on race. *Jesus has destroyed the barrier!* Now that I am more than twice that old, I look back and see a sadder and more poignant image: When I walked among those stones that day, I was alone. There was no "two" for Jesus to make into "one." There was only me.

The truth is that exclusion does not harm only the ones who are sent away. The vestiges of historical segregation in our country—in our neighborhoods and our churches, in our shopping malls and our schools—also harm the ones who stay.

There can be no comparison of the suffering, of course. Trying to claim an injury to White people smacks of the abhorrent condescension of the Southern plantation owners who told their enslaved field hands that their own burden of budgeting and decision-making was heavier than the work of sweating in the cotton fields. How false, and how gross.

But White suffering is nevertheless real. "White people . . . have suffered greatly," wrote Wendell Berry in *The Hidden Wound*. Derrick Bell said, "Racial segregation afflicts white children with a lifelong mental and emotional handicap that is as destructive to whites as the required strictures of segregation are to Negroes." Heather McGhee added, "There is a psychic and emotional cost to the tightrope white people walk, clutching their identity as good people when all around them is suffering they don't know how to stop." Elsewhere, McGhee spoke of the "moral cost of racism that millions of white people bear." That cost is a result of the guilt we do not know how to staunch.

And there is a cost, too, in the loss of intimate cross-racial relationships we do not know how to reforge. Even when I traveled across the world to spend six months in Malawi, and certainly since I've returned, I have felt the sting of racialized loneliness. This is not a grievance that seems to have occurred to many White people in the nineteenth century. When Oregon's governor ordered, in 1856, that all the members of Oregon's First Nations must move to reservations, Oregon City's people grieved not the loss of their neighbors but the interruption in their salmon supply. None of the White residents knew how to fish. And no one in nineteenth-century Oregon City seems to have grieved the absence of Jacob Vanderpool either. But today, perhaps, we can begin to recognize that by breaking these relationships, many of us have lost out on the gifts, talents, resources, abilities, and perspectives of so many other members of the human race.

This is an Oregonian problem, and it is an American problem, and it is a Christian problem.

In his introduction to *The Christian Imagination: Theology and the Origins of Race*, Willie James Jennings told two stories. One was of White missionaries who awkwardly entered his mother's back garden one day and stiffly invited her to come to their church, two hundred yards away. The young Jennings could not understand why the men did not already know about the deep character of his mother's faith. "Why did these men not know me," Jennings wondered, ". . . and not know the multitude of other black Christians who filled the neighborhood that surrounded that church?"

The other story he told is of the sincere "fatherly love" he experienced from the White, Dutch Reformed professors at Calvin College after he preached his first sermon. Their embrace was, for

Jennings, "the exercise of an imaginative capacity to redefine the social, to claim, to embrace, to join, to desire." But the fact that this moment of appreciation was so unusual—as opposed to the more typical not-knowing displayed by the White missionaries from next door—is what "indicates," for Jennings, "something deeply, painfully amiss." Christianity in the West, Jennings wrote, has largely lost its capacity for cross-racial intimacy.

I tried to figure out how to reach across the chasm. I considered starting a Be the Bridge group, but it requires a co-leader of color, and I did not have one. I attended a virtual meeting of Coming to the Table, a network that brings descendants of enslaved people together with descendants of enslavers. I joined the Clackamas County chapter of Showing Up for Racial Justice. But I cannot say that I was a very good member of these groups. Is it just a lame excuse when I say that the evening meetings were difficult to cram into my schedule of driving four children to baseball practices and band concerts?

I tried to reach out to people of color, just to talk. A few responded, and for their generosity I am most grateful. But most did not, and I can't say I blame them. Maybe there was something wrong with the way that I asked. Maybe they were wary of being tokenized. Or maybe they were simply tired of dragging up their racial trauma, one more time, to satisfy one more White person's curiosity.

"Understanding racism's harm upon White people is not 'a reason to feel sorry for white people or to view them as "victims," ' " Chanequa Walker-Barnes said, quoting Shannon Sullivan. Walker-Barnes continued, "Taking responsibility for the way in which

White culture and White racial identity have been formed and distorted ought to be the primary work of White Christians who claim to desire racial reconciliation and racial justice." So I tried to focus on that. To take responsibility for my own identity and find ways to speak into my own culture. Still, it made me sad to have to do it by myself.

Then I met Taylor Stewart.

The email came forwarded to me through Nancy Slavin, the leader of the Showing Up for Racial Justice chapter I had joined. In spite of my very marginal involvement with the group, Nancy and I had become friends. She was a writer too, and we'd exchanged work. She knew I was researching Jacob Vanderpool—in fact, she was the one who'd sent me the picture of the Jacob Vanderpool sign at the Oregon City Juneteenth celebration. So when Nancy received an email from Taylor Stewart indicating his interest in Jacob Vanderpool, she passed it on to me.

Taylor is a young Black man from Oregon who took a trip, as a college student, to the American South. He was deeply moved by the National Memorial for Peace and Justice, which remembers the thousands of African Americans lynched by White mobs. Taylor returned to Oregon determined to continue the project of memorializing injustice. He founded the Oregon Remembrance Project and spent three years organizing the community of Coos Bay, Oregon, in setting up a monument to Alonzo Tucker, who was lynched there in 1902. And now Taylor wanted to turn his attention to Jacob Vanderpool.

"I've been looking forward to this meeting all week!" Taylor told me with a big smile on his face as he popped into view in the Zoom window on my computer.

"Me too!" I exclaimed. I couldn't believe it; five years after I picked Jacob Vanderpool's name out of the clear blue sky and decided I wanted to find out more about him, here was someone who cared about him as much as I did. And not only that, but he was inviting me to join him in the project of creating a lasting memorial to Jacob Vanderpool in Oregon City.

"I can't wait to get started!" I gushed.

Over the next weeks and months, as I continued to meet with Taylor Stewart and others in Oregon City who wanted to join the memorial work, I was awed by the scope of his vision. He had created a four-phase plan for the state of Oregon. Phase one, which he was currently working on, involved rallying communities throughout the state to memorialize specific victims of racial injustice in Oregon. In phase two, Taylor hoped to create tangible change for the Oregonians of color today, including—to take just *one* of Taylor's lofty but, in his eyes, wholly achievable goals as an example—abolishing the state's death penalty. Phase three would include creating a museum to tell these stories. And in phase four, Taylor wanted the only state in America with a history of formally excluding Black people to begin to actively recruit and support people of color to live and work here.

Every time I attended a meeting with Taylor, I was impressed by the joy that emanated from him even as we grappled with such heavy history. I never saw him shame the largely White Oregon communities he worked with. Rather, he celebrated the gifts each person brought to the group. Once, he told us about a project in Grants Pass, Oregon, which had been an official sundown town.

"Now Grants Pass is excited about becoming a sunrise town!" Taylor told us.

"Sunrise Town—what a great name!" Liz Hannum replied. Liz worked for the Downtown Oregon City Association.

"Wish I could claim it!" Taylor responded. "A sixty-nine-year-old White trucker in Grants Pass came up with that. Isn't that awesome?"

That seemed to get Liz's wheels turning. "You know," she mused, "we're going to start an initiative to have Oregon City businesses sign a pledge to be kind and fair. Maybe we should call it the Vanderpool Contract!"

"I love it!" Taylor said.

I loved it too.

"What I love about doing this work," Taylor went on, "is that when we memorialize a victim of injustice, we add another chapter to their story. Jacob Vanderpool's story did not end in 1851. Now that we're working on this, we are continuing his story. This will become a tipping point for Oregon City—a marker of the moment that Oregon City came together and decided to remember what happened in the past, repair it, and bring it to redemption."

The next time I heard from Taylor, he had moved up phase four of his long-term plan for Oregon. He now wants to begin his statewide goal of recruiting and retaining people of color right here in Oregon City.

The culmination of these projects is probably still years away. The land where Vanderpool's business once stood now belongs to the Confederated Tribes of the Grand Ronde, and they have their own stories to tell. There will be years of demolition and environmental cleanup and construction of something new. Taylor's other goals— abolishing the death penalty, creating a museum, recruiting people of color to live in Oregon—will take time and money and collaboration and hard work.

I recognize that I, too, am still at the beginning of my own journey. I am still learning to think again about my own White supremacy. Still awkwardly working out how to step into the process of repair and redemption. Still learning to forge connections with my larger community. Still making mistakes and having to relearn the movement of repentance all over again.

But I have this hope: Someday, Black Oregonians like Taylor Stewart and Zachary Stocks will stand together with the descendants of the Clackamas Tribe and with the descendants of Oregon's early White pioneers. All will stand together, within reach of the spray from the falls of the Willamette. Together, we will unveil a memorial* —a testament to the pain and tragedy the site has seen. An imperfect reckoning for the incalculable losses of the tribe and the injustice done to Jacob Vanderpool and those like him. An acknowledgment of what the city's White residents lost as well when they banished all others from their midst. A nod to the future, to the kind of place we want to create next: a place where all can become, together, the beloved community.

Jacob Vanderpool's story is not over. Neither is mine. Neither is Oregon City's. A new chapter, for all of us, is just getting started.

---

*While I wait for this day, a humbler memorial has taken shape: My daughter recently painted the bird from Jacob Vanderpool's ad into a mural of famous Oregonians in the hallway at her high school.

∽∅∼

As my research on Vanderpool's life was drawing to a close, my family had the opportunity to take the trip of a lifetime. My husband, Jeremy, had won from the Lilly Foundation a Clergy Renewal grant, a coveted award among pastors that pays a generous stipend for a sabbatical project of the pastor's choosing. Jeremy's grant proposal outlined three adventures, all centered on the idea of gathering with "church on the margins." We would travel to visit West African pastors in Cameroon; we would pay a visit to the United Kingdom to meet John Swinton, a professor at the University of Aberdeen who works on theology of disability; and we would take a road trip to uncover my husband's ancestral roots on the Pine Ridge Reservation in South Dakota.

It was an ambitious proposal. And in every way, the trip exceeded our expectations.

I had come a long way since the day, five years earlier, when I sat with my children in Starbucks and couldn't figure out how to talk with them about race. Now we sat together in Cameroon and talked about how it felt for them to be, for the first time in their lives, in the racial minority. We talked about the whiplash of moving from among the formerly colonized to the former colonizers as we flew from Africa to Europe, and we observed the economic consequences of colonialism still visible on both continents. We journeyed to the heart of the North American continent and showed our children one piece of their own racial heritage.

And everywhere we went, we attended church. In Cameroon,

we worshipped with refugees from the Central African Republic, who gathered in a dirt-floor shed to sing and dance in one of the most expansively joyful worship services I have ever participated in. We shuffled in line with other tourists to go to Evensong at Westminster Abbey, where I gazed up at the immense stained glass windows and reflected on all the things that had happened outside those walls over the past one thousand years, while every day of those years, people gathered in that building to pray and to sing. We found the church that had been started by my husband's great-great-grandfather, the first Lakota Presbyterian pastor on the Pine Ridge Reservation. In that church, we even got to sing hymns out of the Dakota-language hymnbook, our mouths stretching across unfamiliar syllables to form the language that had been spoken in that place since time began.

In that little Lakota Presbyterian church, the pastor invited my husband to come up and explain why we were there. "I'm a direct descendant of Samuel Rouillard, who built this church," Jeremy explained. He was interrupted by a little old lady with an oxygen tube trailing from her nostrils.

"I've been coming to this church ever since I was born," she called from the back row, "and I remember your people!" She raised a withered hand and pointed shakily at the chancel. "I can see your people now, standing right behind you."

Your people . . . standing right behind you. The book of Hebrews says that we are all surrounded by "a great cloud of witnesses." All our people, standing right behind us. No longer—to borrow the apostle Paul's language—do our people "see through a glass, darkly"; now they see clearly, having come face-to-face with the love of God. John McLoughlin, Theophilus Magruder, Thomas Nelson, Ezra Fisher—wherever they are now, I believe that all of them have had the opportunity to think again. To think bigger. To think differently. I like to imagine that even now, with the eternal perspective they lacked when they walked here on earth, they are cheering us on, encouraging us to turn from whatever mistakes they made.

I like to think they're excited to see what's going to happen next in the place we make.

Epilogue

After Repentance

"But how much do you like white people?"

The question seemed strange.

"I'm not much thrilled with the culture we've created."

"Yeah, okay. But how about white people?"

I didn't know what he was driving at.

"I like white people just fine," I said. "I mean, after all, I am one."

"That's what I mean," he chuckled. "That's good. That's good. If you hate your own people you can't be a very good person. You have to love your own people even if you hate what they do." He gestured toward the mug on the table. "Here. Drink your coffee."

—Kent Nerburn, *Neither Wolf nor Dog: On Forgotten Roads with an Indian Elder*

I don't know if I will ever be finished repenting of White supremacy in this lifetime.

I still grieve the stray thoughts that sometimes flit across my brain, the racialized assumptions I still catch myself making, the power structures I still participate in and benefit from. And that's just me. What of my people? Will we, as a people, ever finish repenting of the destruction we have wreaked on so many other cultures around the globe? Will we ever finish repairing what we've broken and returning what we stole?

Maybe not. Or maybe it will take hundreds of years—as long as it took to inflict all the damage in the first place. But even here, at the very beginning of my own journey of repentance, I wonder what it would look like to arrive.

This thought came to me recently as I was reading Cornel West and Richard Twiss side by side. I noticed that both writers were (it seemed to me) primarily addressing their own peoples. In *Race Matters*, West urged Black people to love themselves. In *Rescuing the Gospel from the Cowboys*, Twiss encouraged American Indians to bring their cultural identities to their practice of Christian faith. This observation made me question if it would even be possible to speak a direct and encouraging word to my own people as a group. Would it be possible to affirm something about White identity—as West does for Black identity and Twiss does for American Indian identity—without slipping back into the repugnance of winner-take-all White supremacy? Is there something positive and God-given that White culture can bring to the project of our shared humanity?

Another way to ask the question is this: Once the legacy of hatefulness is burned away, what remains?

Decades ago, in a Wheaton College chapel service, I heard a Ugandan pastor whose name I can no longer recall describe life under the cruel dictatorship of Idi Amin. Amin's rule was exceptionally violent, with hundreds of thousands of people slaughtered, and exceptionally hard on Christians, with churches shuttered and their people frequently executed. In the midst of all that, the pastor said, he'd had a vision.

"The Lord showed me he was going to use the Ugandan church to come together and pray for Idi Amin to be removed, and that's how the dictatorship was going to end," the pastor said, except of course I can no longer remember his exact words. "Each Christian denomination in Uganda would come, and as they came together, they would all be one in purpose while each retained their own individual character. The Presbyterians would still be Presbyterians, and the Catholics would still be Catholics, and the Methodists would still be Methodists, but they would all come together as one."

And that's exactly what happened: Despite intense persecution, prayer networks sprang up all around the country, different groups coming together to pray for deliverance from Idi Amin, who was eventually overthrown.

What I found so striking about the pastor's story was the idea that entities that had splintered apart—in this case, Christian denominations that had fractured in Europe during the Protestant Reformation and then exported their differences to the missions they founded in Uganda and around the globe—could later be reunited with *one purpose* yet *retaining their distinct characters*. Whenever I read Jesus's prayer for the unity of the church, the last prayer he prayed before his crucifixion, I grieve the fact that the Christian church has now been split into thirty thousand denominations and counting. It fascinates me to imagine that when God draws the church together again, as happened in Uganda, it might not be in order to reforge a single uniform entity but rather to create a new kind of thing: one in purpose, yet gloriously multi-hued in nature.

I wonder if something similar might happen with the tribes, nations, and races we've created. Human societies have splintered apart, with war and oppression dividing one people group from another. Could there be a future in which humanity reunites not by returning to a single uniform state but by cooperating around a shared purpose while retaining each community's own unique, precious, and indispensable identity?

The gospel is full of paradoxes, and so, I think, two things can be true at the same time. We can all be *one* in Christ Jesus, who brings down the proud and lifts the humble. As Galatians 3:28 says, "There is neither Jew nor Gentile, neither slave nor free, nor is there male and female, for you are all one in Christ Jesus." All are welcome into citizenship in the heavenly city, equal in status as children of the Most High God. But this other thing can also be true: Our identity remains, even after everything untrue, unreal, and unholy has been washed away. After all, the book of Revelation tells us that in heaven, there will be "a great multitude that no one could count, from every nation, tribe, people and language." An Athabascan chief in Richard Twiss's book said, "I . . . liked the picture in Revelation where all the nations and tribes and tongues were there, and I would always think, *Oh, the tribes—wow! So there is going to be our tribal people there.*" One in purpose, yet even on into eternity, retaining something of the distinct and unique nature of who we are now.

Judging by the number of different insects that roam the earth and the sheer variety of fish that swim in the sea, I think it's safe to say that God *likes* diversity. God's goal has never been to wave a magic wand and make us all the same. But wouldn't it be just like

God to take something that humans have created for our own self-ish purposes—nations that war against nations, people groups that turn against other people groups—and turn the system upside down, shake all the evil out, and set it free to become something pure and beautiful and good?

Maybe the word I want to speak to my own people, if such a statement can even be made, is simply this: Let us become a community of humble, joyful servants, no longer seeking to oppress, to save, or to control. Let us simply empty ourselves of ill-gotten wealth and power and status, for the good of the whole.

For we have much work to do. The planet is hurting. Children are dying. Lies are flourishing. In the face of all this, racial repentance cannot be the end. It must be the beginning. The goal of repentance is to clear the logjam of hostility, making way for the glorious, multi-channeled stream of humanity, each tongue, tribe, and nation coursing together, bearing their own unique and valuable gifts toward our common aim: that the mighty river of God's justice and righteousness might flow.

"There is a river," the psalmist wrote, "whose streams make glad the city of God."

Ezekiel the prophet saw this river in a vision: rushing out in all directions from the thresholds of the temple, growing deeper as it flows. Where the river runs, Ezekiel reports, everything will *live*. Fishermen will line its shores, pulling fish of all kinds from its sparkling waters. Fruit trees of all kinds will stretch their branches over the water, sending their roots deep into its banks. The leaves of the trees will not wither, and their fruit will not fail. These trees are watered by the very sanctuary of God so their fruit will feed the hungry and their leaves will heal the hurting.

From his exile on the island of Patmos, John the apostle saw this river too. In John's vision, the river of the water of life flows clear as crystal, straight down from the throne of God along the middle of the city's widest street. John's river, too, yields plentiful fruit orchards. On the banks of John's river, too, the leaves of the fruit trees heal the nations.

Behold! cries the voice of the One on the throne. *There will be no more death or mourning or crying or pain, for the old order of things has passed away. . . . I am making everything new!*

Let the river flow.

Discussion Questions

Introduction–Prologue
1. Toni Morrison urges us to consider both the "slaves" and the "masters" of slavery. Which has been your focus so far?
2. What thoughts come to mind about the place and time that you call home?

Chapter One
1. What responsibility does John McLoughlin bear for what happened to Jacob Vanderpool?
2. What do you know about how your family or local place may have intersected with slavery or White supremacy?

Chapter Two
1. How do you feel about the idea that ignorance can be a sin of omission? In what way can we remedy ignorance?
2. How have you given or received empathy? What can we do to gain more empathy for others?

Chapter Three
1. How does the history of slavery in the United States change how you think about racism?
2. What patterns of harm have you noticed in your family or place that passed down through generations?

Chapter Four
1. What have you received, good or bad, from generations who came before?
2. How should we navigate our associations with groups whose actions we don't entirely agree with?

Chapter Five
1. How do conflicts of interest influence our correctional system and our perception of justice?

2. What is the relationship between people and your local land—now and in the past?

3. What do you know about the Indigenous people who first lived (and perhaps still live) in your area?

Chapter Six

1. How do the ideas of state- and church-sponsored White supremacy still influence modern society?

2. What is your experience with committing or receiving acts of "everyday" racism?

3. How have you encountered forgiveness, and how did it free you to do better?

Chapter Seven

1. In the incomprehensible number of injustices we walk (or scroll) by daily, how do we decide what to pay attention to and what to fight for?

2. How should we treat those whose past behaviors we now condemn?

Chapter Eight

1. When did you regret staying silent or when did someone else's silence cause harm?

2. How do you respond to the beliefs of the gathered community of the church?

3. How did someone you disagreed with help you change your mind?

Chapter Nine

1. What should we do with plaques and statues that still memorialize White supremacy? How might we tell a truer story?

2. What stands out to you about Jacob Vanderpool's life after the trial?

Chapter Ten

1. When you consider your communities, where might God be at work doing a new thing?

2. How will you continue to build an accurate understanding of the place you call home and contribute to its good?

Epilogue

1. Is it possible to finish "repenting of White supremacy"?

2. How might the image of the river of God's justice and healing inspire our communities today?

Acknowledgments

If I had the space to thank every person I've ever known, I would. Every word, every prayer, every act of welcome has been a healing gift. Thank you all.

Two people saw that the writing vocation belonged to me, and told me so. Thank you, Sooz Watson and Amy Silbernagel McCaffree, for encouraging me to begin. And thank you, Rebecca Heidkamp, for asking the question.

The Master of Fine Arts program at Seattle Pacific University changed my life. Thank you to Greg and Suzanne Wolfe, Scott Cairns, Susanne Paola Antonetta, Bob Cording, Robert Clark, Gina Ochsner, Ann Gillespie, Chris Hoke, and many others, for making the program what it was for me. Thank you to my workshop partners, including Cat Ricketts, Arthur Boers, and Sarah Orner; those who workshopped pieces of this manuscript, including Janay Garrick, Elise Tegegne, and Tricia Peters; and especially Amy Peterson and Cara Strickland, who walked with me the whole way. Special thanks to Lauren Winner for calling this book into being and pouring so much incisive wisdom into its early drafts.

If prayer is the greater work, as Oswald Chambers said, then the people who have done the greatest work on this manuscript include Marie and John Sanderson, Dontá McGilvery, Chris Warren, Sid Sudiacal, Nicolle Maurer, Kirk McCall, Bethany Everson Na, Cris Polk, Jonathan Tremaine Thomas, Kelly Noll, Tanya

Stojanovich, Carolita Feiring, Wade Van Buskirk, Sylvia Totzke, and Catherine and Maria Haras. Thank you, Pamela Havey Lau, for reminding me of the practicality of prayer, and Luci Shaw, for telling me to listen to my angel. Thank you especially to Christy and Eben Polk and Alex and Mae Moore for listening with me at every stage of the journey.

In diving into a research project of this size, I relied upon the expertise of Zachary Stocks of Oregon Black Pioneers, Ross Sutherland of the Bush House Museum, Jo Lynn Dow and Johnnie Heintz of the Clackamas County Historical Society, Nancy Slavin of the Clackamas County chapter of Showing Up for Racial Justice, Marianne Ryder, Joan Duffy, Nathan Luis Cartagena, Rich Schmidt, Katie and John Withum, Abram Neumann, Jeff Miller, and others. Gerald and Dale Baugh provided enormous amounts of background knowledge, and I am sorry I could not include more of your stories. Huge thanks to Peter Lucas-Roberts for taking an early and lasting interest in this project.

People who read early drafts or pieces of this book and provided helpful feedback include Sarah Head, Beth Killian, Robert Monson, Lisa Colón DeLay, David Toth, Kristine Aragon-Bruce, and Ryan Browning. Thank you especially to Taylor Stewart of Oregon Remembrance Project for understanding my vision and inspiring me with your own.

Many people provided invaluable encouragement. Huge thanks to Malika Lee, Cara Meredith, Leigh Ann Erickson, Mindy Haidle, Marc Schelske, Lynne Baab, Greg Atkinson, Matt Milliner, Leslie Leyland Fields, Shawn and Maile Smucker, Cornelia Signeur, Stella Kasirye, Marlena Prosper Graves, DeeAnn Johnson, Liz

Garcia, Lynda Bogel, Neida Rendon, Stephanie Gehring Ladd, Amy Ickes, Amy Rouillard, Jane Scharl, Charlotte Donlon, and the people of Alliance Charter Academy and Oak Hills Presbyterian Church for helping me out and cheering me on. Thank you, Don and Karen Gissell, for the use of your fabulous house. Special thanks to Laurel Neal for your abounding faith in me.

Thank you, Chanté Griffin and Velynn Brown, for welcoming me. Thank you, Mary Lane Potter, for your generous feedback, and thank you to all the members of the Collegeville Institute's Writing Spirit, Writing Faith workshop, especially Laurie Skiba, Laura Hudson, Libby Sutherland, and Chelsey Hillyer for continuing with me.

Thank you to Kevin Robinson, Vicky Pasquantonio, Bonnie Rubrecht, Quintard Taylor, Andrea Palpant Dilley, Jen Johnson, Chara Donahue, Diana Whitney, Dan Bowman, Stina Kielsmeier-Cook, and everyone else who partnered with me to put my words in front of people. Thank you, JD Tyler, for your generous and beautiful work on my website.

Thank you, Michael Yao, for the book club sessions that masqueraded as psychiatrist appointments. Thank you, Rachel Reed, for holding everything so gently.

To Paul Pastor, my first editor: Thank you for taking a risk on me, trusting me with this work, and always pointing me to love the reader. To Estee Zandee, my second editor, thank you for the hard work you put in to bring this project to completion. To the entire team at WaterBrook and Penguin Random House, especially Linda Washington, Johanna Inwood, Helen Macdonald, Luverta Reames, Lisa Grimenstein, Cara Iverson, Carrie Krause, Melanie

Barreiro, and many others: I'm so thankful for each and every one of you. Finally, I'm so incredibly grateful to my agent, Keely Boeving. Without your steadfast enthusiasm, I would have given up long ago.

To my mother, Nancy Lucas Williams: Thank you for everything, from financial and childcare support to tireless prayers, but especially for showing me how to walk the path of faith and the path of the artist. To my brother Joe: Thank you for educating me, and to Abe, thank you for being who you are. To my children, Abby, Josiah, Levi, and Isaac: Thank you for showing me what is important about the world and for calling me back to it. To my husband, Jeremy: Thank you for being my first reader, my gentlest critic, and my most faithful friend. You're the one I want, always, along on this ride.

To God be the glory.

For Further Reading

(An Incomplete List)

Alexie, Sherman, *The Absolutely True Diary of a Part-Time Indian.*

Angelou, Maya, *I Know Why the Caged Bird Sings.*

Baldwin, James, *Notes of a Native Son.*

Barber, Leroy, with Velma Maia Thomas, *Red, Brown, Yellow, Black, White: Who's More Precious in God's Sight?*

Bell, Derrick, *Silent Covenants: Brown v. Board of Education and the Unfulfilled Hopes for Racial Reform.*

Berry, Wendell, *The Hidden Wound.*

Blow, Charles M., *Fire Shut Up in My Bones: A Memoir.*

Brown, Austin Channing, *I'm Still Here: Black Dignity in a World Made for Whiteness.*

Charles, Mark, and Soong-Chan Rah, *Unsettling Truths: The Ongoing, Dehumanizing Legacy of the Doctrine of Discovery.*

Chung, Nicole, *All You Can Ever Know: A Memoir.*

Cisneros, Sandra, *The House on Mango Street.*

Coates, Ta-Nehisi, *Between the World and Me.*

Coleman, Kenneth Robert, *Dangerous Subjects: James D. Saules and the Rise of Black Exclusion in Oregon.*

Deloria, Jr., Vine, *For This Land: Writings on Religion in America.*

Douglass, Frederick, *Narrative of the Life of Frederick Douglass, An American Slave.*

Dungy, Camille T., *Black Nature: Four Centuries of African American Nature Poetry.*

Emerson, Michael O., and Christian Smith, *Divided by Faith: Evangelical Religion and the Problem of Race in America.*

Erdrich, Louise, *The Night Watchman.*

Fields, Karen E., and Barbara J. Fields, *Racecraft: The Soul of Inequality in American Life.*

Flowers, Ebony, *Hot Comb.*

Hamad, Ruby, *White Tears/Brown Scars: How White Feminism Betrays Women of Color.*

Harper, Lisa Sharon, *Fortune: How Race Broke My Family and the World and How to Repair It All.*

hill, myisha t, *Heal Your Way Forward: The Co-Conspirator's Guide to an Antiracist Future.*

Hosseini, Khaled, *The Kite Runner.*

Hughes, Langston, *Selected Poems.*

Irving, Debby, *Waking Up White and Finding Myself in the Story of Race.*

Jennings, Willie James, *The Christian Imagination: Theology and the Origins of Race.*

Kendi, Ibram X., *How to Be an Antiracist.*

Kincaid, Jamaica, *A Small Place.*

Kwon, Duke L., and Gregory Thompson, *Reparations: A Christian Call for Repentance and Repair.*

McCaulley, Esau, *Reading While Black: African American Biblical Interpretation as an Exercise in Hope.*

McGhee, Heather, *The Sum of Us: What Racism Costs Everyone and How We Can Prosper Together.*

McLagan, Elizabeth, *A Peculiar Paradise: A History of Blacks in Oregon, 1788–1940.*

McNeil, Brenda Salter, *Becoming Brave: Finding the Courage to Pursue Racial Justice Now.*

Milliner, Matthew J., *The Everlasting People: G. K. Chesterton and the First Nations.*

Moore, Osheta, *Dear White Peacemakers: Dismantling Racism with Grit and Grace.*

Morgan, Edmund S., *American Slavery, American Freedom.*

Morrison, Dorothy Nafus, *Outpost: John McLoughlin and the Far Northwest.*

Morrison, Latasha, *Be the Bridge: Pursuing God's Heart for Racial Reconciliation.*

Morrison, Toni, *Playing in the Dark: Whiteness and the Literary Imagination.*

Nayeri, Daniel, *Everything Sad Is Untrue.*

Nerburn, Kent, *Neither Wolf nor Dog: On Forgotten Roads with an Indian Elder.*

Nokes, R. Gregory, *Breaking Chains: Slavery on Trial in the Oregon Territory.*

Nye, Naomi Shihab, *19 Varieties of Gazelle: Poems of the Middle East.*

Oluo, Ijeoma, *So You Want to Talk About Race.*

Perry, Imani, *South to America: A Journey Below the Mason-Dixon to Understand the Soul of a Nation.*

Ramsey, Jarold, ed., *Coyote Was Going There: Indian Literature of the Oregon Country.*

Rankine, Claudia, *Citizen: An American Lyric.*

Rodriguez, Richard, *Brown: The Last Discovery of America.*

Saad, Layla F., *Me and White Supremacy: Combat Racism, Change the World, and Become a Good Ancestor.*

Satrapi, Marjane, *Persepolis: The Story of a Childhood.*

Smith, Clint, *How the Word Is Passed: A Reckoning with the History of Slavery Across America.*

Smith, Zadie, *On Beauty: A Novel.*

Swanson, David W., *Rediscipling the White Church: From Cheap Diversity to True Solidarity.*

Tisby, Jemar, *The Color of Compromise: The Truth About the American Church's Complicity in Racism.*

Twiss, Richard, *Rescuing the Gospel from the Cowboys: A Native American Expression of the Jesus Way.*

Walker-Barnes, Chanequa, *I Bring the Voices of My People: A Womanist Vision for Racial Reconciliation.*

Ward, Jesmyn, *Men We Reaped.*

Ward, Jesmyn, ed., *The Fire This Time: A New Generation Speaks About Race.*

West, Cornel, *Race Matters.*

Wilkerson, Isabel, *The Warmth of Other Suns: The Epic Story of America's Great Migration.*

Winner, Lauren, *The Dangers of Christian Practice: On Wayward Gifts, Characteristic Damage, and Sin.*

Yang, Gene Luen, *American Born Chinese.*

Notes

Epigraph

ix   *"No free Negro, or Mulatto":* "Transcribed 1857 Oregon Constitution,"
Oregon State Archives, https://sos.oregon.gov/archives/exhibits/
constitution/Documents/transcribed-1857-oregon-constitution.pdf.

ix   *"The only thing about Oregon that is unique":* Walidah Imarisha, "Why
Aren't There More Black People in Oregon? A Hidden History,"
presentation to Diverse and Empowered Employees of Portland,
May 29, 2014, 22:05, www.youtube.com/watch?v=7Lcm1LDZZXg&t
=2965s.

Author's Note

xvii   *"shared culture and history":* Eve L. Ewing, "I'm a Black Scholar Who
Studies Race. Here's Why I Capitalize 'White,'" *Zora,* July 1, 2020,
https://zora.medium.com/im-a-black-scholar-who-studies-race-here-s
-why-i-capitalize-white-f94883aa2dd3.

xvii   *"respect, pride, and celebration":* Ewing, "I'm a Black Scholar."

xvii   *Kwame Anthony Appiah:* Kwame Anthony Appiah, "The Case for Capi-
talizing the *B* in Black," *The Atlantic,* June 18, 2020, www.theatlantic
.com/ideas/archive/2020/06/time-to-capitalize-blackand-white/
613159.

xvii   *Nell Irvin Painter:* Nell Irvin Painter, "Why 'White' Should Be Capital-
ized, Too" *The Washington Post,* July 22, 2020, www.washingtonpost
.com/opinions/2020/07/22/why-white-should-be-capitalized.

xvii   *Imani Perry:* Imani Perry, "A Note from the Author," *South to America:*

A Journey Below the Mason-Dixon to Understand the Soul of a Nation (New York: HarperCollins, 2022), xi.

xvii   *Leaving the* w *uncapitalized:* Ewing, "I'm a Black Scholar."

Introduction

xix   *"Let us take a knife":* Langston Hughes, "Tired," *The Collected Poems of Langston Hughes,* ed. Arnold Rampersad and David Roessel (New York: Vintage Classics, 1995), 135.

xx   *the only person ever expelled from Oregon:* Mitchell S. Jackson, "Oregon," *Four Hundred Souls: A Community History of African America, 1619-2019,* ed. Ibram X. Kendi and Keisha N. Blain (New York: Random House, 2022), 210.

xxii   *"The scholarship that looks into the mind, imagination":* Toni Morrison, *Playing in the Dark: Whiteness and the Literary Imagination* (New York: Vintage Books, 1992), 11–12.

xxiii   *The Christian Imagination:* Willie James Jennings, *The Christian Imagination: Theology and the Origins of Race* (New Haven: Yale University Press, 2010).

xxiii   *The Color of Compromise:* Jemar Tisby, *The Color of Compromise: The Truth About the American Church's Complicity in Racism* (Grand Rapids, Mich.: Zondervan, 2019).

xxiv   *the kindness of God:* See Romans 2:4.

Prologue

xxv   *First came the lava:* The science behind these descriptions comes from "Willamette Falls Geology: A Story of Two Floods," Willamette Falls Legacy Project, April 20, 2017, www.willamettefallslegacy.org/willamette-falls-geology-story-two-floods.

xxvi   *the ancient hero Coyote:* Jarold Ramsey, ed., *Coyote Was Going There: Indian Literature of the Oregon Country* (Seattle: University of Washington Press, 1980), 93.

Chapter One: The Founder

4 *"superb specimen of man" with "magnificent physical proportions"*: Frederick V. Holman, *Dr. John McLoughlin: The Father of Oregon* (Cleveland, Ohio: The Arthur H. Clark Company, 1907), 25; accessed by Project Gutenberg, www.gutenberg.org/files/36146/36146-h/36146-h.htm #Page_25.

4 *"White-Headed Eagle"*: Cassandra Tate, "McLoughlin, John (1784–1857)," HistoryLink.org, September 24, 2013, www.historylink.org/File/10617.

4 *"the Czar of the West," whose "rule was imperial"*: Samuel Asahel Clarke, "Life and Times of Dr. John McLoughlin," *Pioneer Days of Oregon History* (Portland: J.K. Gill, 1905), 211; accessed by Google Books, https://play.google.com/books/reader?id=bUcOAAAAIAAJ&pg=GBS.PA1&hl=en.

4 *"destined by nature"*: "Dr. John McLoughlin's Last Letter to the Hudson's Bay Company, as Chief Factor, in Charge at Fort Vancouver, 1845," *The American Historical Review* 21, no. 1 (October 1915): 120, https://doi.org/10.2307/1836705.

4 *constructed three buildings there*: "Oregon City McLoughlin Historic District," www.oregonmetro.gov/sites/default/files/2014/04/16/walk_there_oregon_city_mcloughlin_historic_district.pdf.

5 *"deep and rich, waiting for their plows"*: Dorothy Nafus Morrison, *Outpost: John McLoughlin and the Far Northwest* (Portland: Oregon Historical Society Press, 1999), 401.

5 *"Almost every tribe . . . can point out"*: Vine Deloria, Jr., "The Coming of the People," *For This Land: Writings on Religion in America* (Oxfordshire: Routledge, 1998), 241.

5 *six longhouses and "numerous" Clowwewalla*: Fred S. Perrine, "Early Days on the Willamette," *The Quarterly of the Oregon Historical Society* 25, no. 4 (December 1924): 295–312, www.jstor.org/stable/20610287.

6 *abundance of salmon and "Nutricious Roots"*: Mathias D. Bergmann, " 'We Should Lose Much by Their Absence': The Centrality of Chinookans and Kalapuyans to Life in Frontier Oregon," *Oregon Historical Quarterly* 109, no. 1 (Spring 2008): 34–59, www.jstor.org/stable/20615823.

6   *"made the arrangements for the execution":* Holman, *Dr. John McLough-lin*, 38.

7   *"house & store":* Morrison, *Outpost*, 388.

7   *"I have Drunk and am Drinking":* Morrison, *Outpost*, 431.

10 *"until such time as the United States of America":* Marie Merriman Brad-ley, "Political Beginnings in Oregon: The Period of the Provisional Government, 1839–1849," *The Quarterly of the Oregon Historical Society* 9, no. 1 (March 1908): 51, www.jstor.org/stable/20609761.

11 *the question of whether Oregon would enter the Union as a slave state:* Greg-ory Nokes, *Breaking Chains: Slavery on Trial in the Oregon Territory* (Corvallis, Ore.: Oregon State University Press, 2013), 2.

12 *"I'm going to Oregon . . . where there'll be no slaves":* John Minto, "Remi-niscences of Honorable John Minto, Pioneer of 1844," *The Quarterly of the Oregon Historical Society* 2, no. 2 (June 1901): 130, www.jstor.org/stable/i20609491.

12 *"Many of those people hated slavery, but":* Elizabeth McLagan, *A Peculiar Paradise: A History of Blacks in Oregon, 1778–1940* (Corvallis, Ore.: Or-egon State University Press, 1980), 29.

12 *the population of Black residents in the Oregon Territory in the 1840s:* Ken-neth Robert Coleman, "Dangerous Subjects: James D. Saules and the Enforcement of the Color Line in Oregon" (PhD diss., Portland State University, 2014), 92, https://doi.org/10.15760/etd.1844.

12 *Ambivalence about the slave issue:* I owe these thoughts to the work of Kenneth Coleman in his book *Dangerous Subjects: James D. Saules and the Rise of Black Exclusion in Oregon* (Corvallis, Ore.: Oregon State University Press, 2017).

13 *"not to establish trade with the Indians":* Peter Hardeman Burnett, *Recol-lections and Opinions of an Old Pioneer* (New York: D. Appleton, 1880), 150.

13 *"felt most vulnerable. Most had traveled":* Coleman, *Dangerous Sub-jects*, 18.

13 *"he would stand for the Indians' rights":* U.S. Congress, United States Of-fice of Indian Affairs, Annual Report of the Commissioner of Indian Af-fairs, 29th Cong., 1st Sess., 182 (1846).

13 *"ought to be transported, together with every other Negro":* Annual Report of the Commissioner of Indian Affairs, 182.

14 *"quit the Territory":* "Oregon History: Chronological Events," *Oregon Blue Book: Almanac and Fact Book,* https://sos.oregon.gov/blue-book/Pages/facts/history/chronology-1543-1850.aspx.

14 *between 1850 and 1860, "at least 14," and possibly as many as 135:* Quintard Taylor, "Slaves and Free Men: Blacks in the Oregon Country, 1840–1860," *Oregon Historical Quarterly* 83, no. 2 (Summer 1982): 167, www.jstor.org/stable/20613841.

14 *"any negro or mulatto" could not "enter into, or reside":* "(1849) Oregon Exclusion Law," *Blackpast,* www.blackpast.org/african-american-history/oregon-exclusion-law-1849.

14 *"We declare that all men, when they form a social compact":* "Transcribed 1857 Oregon Constitution," Oregon State Archives, https://sos.oregon.gov/archives/exhibits/constitution/Documents/transcribed-1857-oregon-constitution.pdf.

15 *"No free Negro":* "Transcribed 1857."

15 *"We are in a new world under the most favorable circumstances":* Greg Nokes, "Peter Burnett (1807–1895)," *Oregon Encyclopedia,* www.oregonencyclopedia.org/articles/burnett_peter#YQgz-ZNue3I.

15 *"was opposed to slavery largely on account of the evil":* Fred Lockley, "Some Documentary Records of Slavery in Oregon," *The Quarterly of the Oregon Historical Society* 17, no. 2 (June 1916): 109, www.jstor.org/stable/20610035.

18 *Jacob Vanderpool: Oregon Statesman,* June 6, 1851, 3, http://statesmanjournal.newspapers.com/image/218147870.

Chapter Two: From Ignorance to Empathy

19 *"[White people] are in effect still trapped":* James Baldwin, "A Letter to My Nephew," *The Progressive Magazine,* December 1, 1962, https://progressive.org/magazine/letter-nephew.

21 *"the Whitest City in America":* Alana Semuels, "The Racist History of Portland, the Whitest City in America," *The Atlantic,* July 22, 2016, www.theatlantic.com/business/archive/2016/07/racist-history-portland/492035.

23 *"How have you managed not to know?":* Layla Saad, *Me and White Su-*

premacy: Combat Racism, Change the World, and Become a Good Ancestor (Chicago: Sourcebooks, 2020), xii.

25 *a well-documented history of racial segregation in schools:* Danielle Dreilinger, "America's Gifted Education Problems Have a Race Problem. Can It Be Fixed?," NBC News, October 14, 2020, www.nbcnews.com/news/education/america-s-gifted-education-programs-have-race-problem-can-it-n1243143.

26 *the taxonomy of humanity concocted by Swedish botanist Carl Linnaeus:* Ibram X. Kendi, *How to Be an Antiracist* (New York: One World, 2019), 41.

27 *Richard Wright's 1937 essay:* Richard Wright, "The Ethics of Living Jim Crow: An Autobiographical Sketch," *The Best American Essays of the Century,* ed. Joyce Carol Oates and Robert Atwan (Boston: Houghton Mifflin, 2000), 159–70.

28 *"quite small":* Wright, "The Ethics," 159.

28 *"I'll rip yo' string gut loose with this bar!":* Wright, "The Ethics," 163.

28 *"It's a wonder they didn't lay her":* Wright, "The Ethics," 164.

28 *"If yuh'd said tha' t' somebody else, yuh might've been":* Wright, "The Ethics," 166.

28 *"mighty, mighty lucky":* Wright, "The Ethics," 167.

31 *"In 1851, Jacob Vanderpool, the black owner of a saloon":* DeNeen L. Brown, "A Look at Oregon's Shameful History as an 'All-White' State," *The Columbian,* June 17, 2017, www.columbian.com/news/2017/jun/17/oregons-shameful-history-as-an-all-white-state.

Chapter Three: The Treasure Hunter

33 *"rape-colored skin":* Caroline Randall Williams, "You Want a Confederate Monument? My Body Is a Confederate Monument," *The New York Times,* June 26, 2020, www.nytimes.com/2020/06/26/opinion/confederate-monuments-racism.html.

34 *"intense discrimination, few job opportunities":* Daniel Alan Livesay, "Children of Uncertain Fortune: Mixed-Race Migration from the West Indies to Britain, 1750–1820" (PhD Diss., University of Michigan, 2010), 2.

34 *20 percent of American ships' crews:* W. Jeffrey Bolster, *Black Jacks: African American Seamen in the Age of Sail,* as cited in Ken Ringle, "Sailors

on the Winds of Change: Book Finds Black Seamen Helped Carry the Cargo of Freedom," *The Washington Post*, May 10, 2012, www .washingtonpost.com/lifestyle/style/sailors-on-the-winds-of-change -book-finds-black-seamen-helped-carry-the-cargo-of-freedom/2012/ 05/10/gIQA7c6eGU_story.html.

34 *The 1850 United States Census:* "United States Census, 1850," database with images, FamilySearch (www.familysearch.org/ark:/61903/1:1: MCTH-8J4, December 23, 2020), Jacob Vanderpool, New York City, New York County, New York, United States; citing family, NARA microfilm publication (Washington, D.C.: National Archives and Records Administration, n.d.).

35 *approximately seven months pregnant:* I calculated this by assuming that Vanderpool did leave New York in January 1850. The census taken in July recorded that Martin was three months old at that time. "United States Census, 1850."

35 *"whites saw blacks as a separate and unequal group":* Leslie M. Harris, "African-Americans in New York City, 1626–1863," *Emory University Department of History Newsletter* 46, August 2001, http://history.emory .edu/newsletter01/newslo1/african.htm.

35 *"strong links between mariners and victuallers":* Derrick Morris and Ken Cozens, "Mariners Ashore in the Eighteenth Century: The Role of Boarding-House Keepers and Victuallers," *The Mariner's Mirror* 103, no. 4 (2017), www.tandfonline.com/doi/full/10.1080/00253359.2017 .1376481?scroll=top&needAccess=true.

36 *"lieutenants, loafers, ladies, lackbrains, and lawyers":* Walt Whitman, "New York Boarding Houses," *Walt Whitman of the New York Aurora, Editor at Twenty-Two: A Collection of Recently Discovered Writings,* ed. Joseph Jay Rubin and Charles H. Brown (State College, Penn.: Bald Eagle Press, 1950), 23, www.sas.upenn.edu/~cavitch/pdf-library/ Rubin_and_Brown_Whitman_New_York_Aurora.pdf.

37 *the first permanent American settlement in the present-day Seattle area:* Darrell Millner, "George Bush of Tumwater: Founder of the First American Colony on Puget Sound," *Washington State Historical Society, Columbia Magazine* 8, no. 4 (Winter 1994–95): 14, www .washingtonhistory.org/wp-content/uploads/2020/04/george-bush -tumwater.pdf.

38 *legal residence specifically and only to George Washington Bush:* "George
   Washington Bush," Black in Oregon: 1840–1870, Oregon Secretary of
   State website, https://sos.oregon.gov/archives/exhibits/black
   -history/Pages/families/bush.aspx.

38 *The Francises were saved from expulsion at the last minute:* Kenneth
   Hawkins, "Abner Hunt 'A.H.' Francis (c. 1812–1872) and Isaac 'I.B.'
   Francis (1798–1856)," *Oregon Encyclopedia,* www.oregonencyclopedia
   .org/articles/francis-abner-h/#Ywe7GuzMLFo.

38 *"We, the undersigned, having leased the 'Main Street House' ":* Oregon
   Statesman, July 8, 1851, 3, https://statesmanjournal.newspapers.com/
   image/81271636.

39 *"dusty and roughly dressed . . . jovial, and also reckless":* E. Ruth Rock-
   wood, "Diary of Rev. George H. Atkinson, D.D. 1847–1858 (Part II.),"
   Oregon Historical Quarterly 40, no. 2 (June 1939): 168–87, www.jstor
   .org/stable/20611184.

41 *friends of President James Madison:* Ralph C. Shanks, Jr., and Janetta
   Thompson Shanks, *Lighthouses and Lifeboats on the Redwood Coast*
   (San Anselmo, Calif.: Costano Books, 1978), 211.

41 *More than a quarter of a million dollars, in today's money, had gone missing:* "Patrick Magruder (1768–1819): 2nd Librarian of Congress
   1807–1815," Biographies, Library of Congress, www.loc.gov/item/
   nr2001008606/patrick-magruder-1768-1819.

41 *As a child, Magruder had seen gold nuggets on display:* Shanks, *Lighthouses and Lifeboats,* 213.

41 *"thousands of dollars' worth of gold dust":* James D. Miller, "Early Oregon Scenes: A Pioneer Narrative (in Three Parts, II)," *Oregon Historical
   Quarterly* 31, no. 2 (June 1930): 165, www.jstor.org/stable/20610551.

42 *the legislative body met at Magruder's house:* Oregon State Archives: Or-
   egon Legislators and Staff Guide, 1845 Meetings (4th Pre-Provisional):
   June 24–July 5, 4, http://records.sos.state.or.us/ORSOSWebDrawer/
   RecordView/6787089.

42 *they appointed him sergeant-at-arms:* Oregon State Archives: Oregon
   Legislators and Staff Guide, 1845 Regular Session (1st Provisional): December 2–19, https://web.archive.org/web/20161227194244/http://
   sos.oregon.gov/archives/Documents/records/legislative/statehood/
   1845-regular-session.pdf.

42 *Territory of Oregon's first secretary of state:* "Earliest Authorities in Oregon," Oregon Blue Book, https://sos.oregon.gov/blue-book/Documents/elections/history-officials.pdf.

42 *The five-dollar coins were pressed with K.M.T.A.W.R.G.S.:* Leslie M. Scott, "Pioneer Gold Money, 1849," *Oregon Historical Quarterly* 33, no. 1 (March 1932): 25–30, www.jstor.org/stable/20610694.

42 *"one of California's wealthiest and most popular pioneer women":* "Dead Woman Leaves Immense Estate to Seven Sons and Daughters," *Oakland Tribune,* September 6, 1909, www.newspapers.com/clip/25151369/oakland-tribune.

43 *"suffering . . . probably induced by a change of diet":* David G. Lewis, "Removal of Four Tribes from the Umpqua Reservation 1855–1856," *Quartux: Journal of Critical Indigenous Anthropology,* June 16, 2021, https://ndnhistoryresearch.com/2021/06/16/removal-of-four-tribes-from-the-umpqua-reservation-1855-1856.

43 *he quit less than three years later:* Shanks, *Lighthouses and Lifeboats,* 213.

44 *father retired there after his resignation:* "Patrick Magruder (1768–1819): 2nd Librarian of Congress 1807–1815," Biographies, Library of Congress, www.loc.gov/item/nr2001008606/patrick-magruder-1768-1819.

44 *a large slave-owning plantation:* Information about the relative size of the Sweden plantation comes from census records of descendants of Magruder's father-in-law, Peterson Goodwyn. In 1830, a descendant of Goodwyn is recorded as enslaving sixty-three persons; by the 1850 census, the number had grown to 117. The Magruders themselves also owned slaves, apart from their connection with the Sweden plantation. In the 1790 census (nine years before Theophilus's birth), twenty-two-year-old Patrick Magruder was listed as enslaving two people, while his father, Samuel, enslaved seventeen.

44 *"did not import shiploads of African slaves":* Edmund S. Morgan, *American Slavery, American Freedom* (New York: Norton, 1975), 133.

45 *"every year it poured a host of new freemen":* Morgan, *American Slavery,* 308.

47 *"These were the men who brought slavery to Virginia":* Morgan, *American Slavery,* 304.

47 *ten million enslaved Black Americans:* J. David Hacker, "From '20. and Odd' to 10 Million: The Growth of the Slave Population in the United

States," *Slavery & Abolition* 41, no. 4 (2020): 840–55, https://doi.org/10.1080/0144039X.2020.1755502.

47 *requiring the deaths of 750,000 American soldiers:* Guy Gugliotta, "New Estimate Raises Civil War Death Toll," *The New York Times*, April 2, 2012, www.nytimes.com/2012/04/03/science/civil-war-toll-up-by-20-percent-in-new-estimate.html.

48 *"the most atrocious offense and alarming behavior":* Armand Francis Lucier, ed., *Journal of Occurrences: Patriot Propaganda on the British Occupation of Boston, 1768–1769* (Westminster, Md.: Heritage Books, 2009), 30–31.

48 *"The whole commerce between master and slave":* Thomas Jefferson, *Notes on the State of Virginia,* cited by Ta-Nehisi Coates, "Thomas Jefferson Was More Than a Man of His Times," *The Atlantic*, December 4, 2012, www.theatlantic.com/national/archive/2012/12/thomas-jefferson-was-more-than-a-man-of-his-times/265850.

49 *the court transcript records: Theophilus Magruder v. Jacob Vanderpool* Case Documents, B 122, Special Collections & University Archives, University of Oregon Libraries, Eugene, Oregon, https://scua.uoregon.edu/repositories/2/resources/1215.

50 *the most ferocious rainstorm its residents had ever seen: Weekly Oregon Statesman,* August 26, 1851, www.newspapers.com/image/218541713.

Chapter Four: From Clenched Fists to Open Hands

51 *"We are writing from the vantage of those who owe":* Duke L. Kwon and Gregory Thompson, *Reparations: A Christian Call for Repentance and Repair* (Grand Rapids, Mich.: Brazos, 2021), 23.

52 *Wendell Berry telling how his own Kentucky relatives:* Wendell Berry, *The Hidden Wound* (Berkeley: Counterpoint, 1989), 5.

53 *When we insist on averting our gaze:* Some of the material in this and other chapters first appeared in "Sitting with the Sins of My White Ancestors," *The Unmooring*, Issue 2, www.theunmooring.org/issue-2.

53 *"Everybody's auntie was an abolitionist":* Esau McCaulley, "Racial Injustice and Public Theology: Panel 2," Conference for Pastoral Theology, October 19, 2021, 36:51, https://centerforpastortheologians.vhx.tv/packages/confronting-racial-injustice-cpt-conference-2021/videos/panel-session-2-fc1zz.

53 *Ta-Nehisi Coates's essay:* Ta-Nehisi Coates, "The Case for Reparations," *The Atlantic,* June 2014, www.theatlantic.com/magazine/
archive/2014/06/the-case-for-reparations/361631.

56 *a chart online showing average sale prices:* Samuel H. Williamson and
Louis P. Cain, "Measuring Slavery in 2020 Dollars," MeasuringWorth
.com, www.measuringworth.com/slavery.php.

59 *labor was worth an average of $180,000 per person:* Williamson and Cain,
"Measuring Slavery."

61 *"In the teaching of American history":* Karen E. Fields and Barbara J.
Fields, *Racecraft: The Soul of Inequality in American Life* (London:
Verso, 2014), 75.

62 *"After committing a small wrong":* "Carl Boone," Reckoning: Facing the
Legacy of Slavery in Kentucky, https://reckoningradio.org/carl-boone
-wpa.

64 *an entry in the book* Colonial Families: George N. MacKenzie and Nelson
Osgood Rhoades, *Colonial Families of the United States of America: In
Which Is Given the History, Genealogy and Armorial Bearings of Colonial
Families Who Settled in the American Colonies from the Time of the Settlement of Jamestown, 13th May, 1607, to the Battle of Lexington, 19th April,
1775,* vol. 7, www.familysearch.org/library/books/viewer/337502/
?offset=9#page=99&viewer=picture&o=search&n=0&q=sprigg.

66 *we each have more than one million tenth cousins:* Brenna M. Henn et al.,
"Cryptic Distant Relatives Are Common in Both Isolated and Cosmo-
politan Genetic Samples," *PLoS ONE* 7, no. 4 (2012), https://doi.org/
10.1371/journal.pone.0034267.

Chapter Five: The Judge

73 *"Oregon City became the Territorial Capital":* Copied from a poster hanging in the Clackamas County courthouse.

75 *"blue ruin":* Henry E. Reed, "William Johnson," *Oregon Historical Quarterly* 34, no. 4 (December 1933): 319, www.jstor.org/stable/20610830.

75 *"rapidly wasting away":* Daniel Lee and Joseph H. Frost, *Ten Years in
Oregon* (New York: J. Collord, 1844), 105, https://books.google.com/
books/about/Ten_Years_in_Oregon.html?id=O3FNAAAAYAAJ.

77 *because they refused to eat bread made from wheat flour:* Anson Dart, "Let-

ter from the Secretary of the Interior," University of Oklahoma College of Law Digital Commons, https://digitalcommons.law.ou.edu/cgi/viewcontent.cgi?article=9357&context=indianserialset.

77 *a crowd had gathered in Oregon City to watch all five Cayuse men hang:* Cassandra Tate, "Cayuse Attack Mission, in What Becomes Known as the Whitman Massacre, on November 29, 1847," Historylink.org, September 24, 2014, www.historylink.org/File/5192.

77 *buried outside the city in unmarked graves:* Ronald B. Lansing, "Whitman Murders Trial," *Oregon Encyclopedia,* www.oregonencyclopedia.org/articles/whitman_massacre_trial/#YZrcHb3MLto.

77 *a woman named Keʒika:* Annual Report of the Commissioner of Indian Affairs to the Secretary of the Interior, United States Bureau of Indian Affairs (Washington: U.S. Government Printing Office, 1850), 212–13, https://play.google.com/store/books/details?id=mJwuAAAAMAAJ&rdid=book-mJwuAAAAMAAJ&rdot=1.

78 *"The objection was sustained":* Thomas Nelson, fl. 1851–1853, [Autograph letter signed] 1851 July 21, Oregon City [to] Cornelia Nelson, https://collections.library.yale.edu/catalog/2054810.

79 *the passage of the Fugitive Slave Act:* Carole Emberton, "Remembering the Sins of Millard Fillmore," *The Washington Post,* January 5, 2018, www.washingtonpost.com/news/made-by-history/wp/2018/01/05/remembering-the-sins-of-millard-fillmore/?outputType=amp.

79 *"pureblood . . . Protestant Anglo-Saxon":* Lorraine Boissoneault, "How the 19th-Century Know Nothing Party Reshaped American Politics," *Smithsonian Magazine,* January 26, 2017, www.smithsonianmag.com/history/immigrants-conspiracies-and-secret-society-launched-american-nativism-180961915.

80 *had arrived in Oregon City on the last day of April 1851:* Sidney Teiser, "The Second Chief Justice of Oregon Territory: Thomas Nelson," *Oregon Historical Quarterly* 48, no. 3 (September 1947): 214–24, www.jstor.org/stable/20611757.

80 *a 1942 essay in the* Oregon Historical Quarterly: Alfred Powers and Mary-Jane Finke, "Survey of First Half-Century of Oregon Hotels," *Oregon Historical Quarterly* 43, no. 3 (September 1942): 232–81, www.jstor.org/stable/20611441.

82 *"twenty woolen coats":* David G. Lewis, "The 1851 Treaty Commission

Journal: The Clackamas Treaty," *Quartux: Journal of Critical Indigenous Anthropology*, November 15, 2017, https://ndnhistoryresearch.com/2017/11/15/the-1851-treaty-commission-journal-the-clackamas-treaty.

83 *the website that hosted the maps:* The maps have since been moved to a slightly more user-friendly website: U.S. Department of the Interior, Bureau of Land Management, www.blm.gov/or/landrecords/survey/ySrvy1.php.

84 *the map just south of Oregon City:* www.blm.gov/or/landrecords/survey/yPlatView1_2.php?path=POR&name=t03os020e_002.jpg.

84 *several little triangles marked "Indian Village":* www.blm.gov/or/landrecords/survey/yPlatView1_2.php?path=POR&name=t02os020e_001.jpg.

86 *"The grid pattern of sellable squares":* Willie James Jennings, *The Christian Imagination: Theology and the Origins of Race* (New Haven: Yale University Press, 2010), 225.

Chapter Six: From Supremacy to Shalom

89 *"How inextricably woven the past is in the present":* Jesmyn Ward, "Introduction," *The Fire This Time* (New York: Scribner, 2016), 9.

90 *"In order to exploit others for your own gain":* Heather McGhee, *The Sum of Us: What Racism Costs Everyone and How We Can Prosper Together* (New York: One World, 2021), 97.

90 *"to invade, search out, capture, vanquish, and subdue":* Mark Charles and Soong-Chan Rah, *Unsettling Truths: The Ongoing, Dehumanizing Legacy of the Doctrine of Discovery* (Downers Grove, Ill.: InterVarsity, 2019), 15.

92 *the Trump White House put out a statement:* "Executive Order on Combating Race and Sex Stereotyping," September 22, 2020, https://trumpwhitehouse.archives.gov/presidential-actions/executive-order-combating-race-sex-stereotyping.

92 *"at least 36 states have adopted or introduced laws or policies":* Cathryn Stout and Thomas Wilburn, "CRT Map: Efforts to Restrict Teaching Racism and Bias Have Multiplied Across the U.S.," Chalkbeat, February 1, 2022, www.chalkbeat.org/22525983/map-critical-race-theory-legislation-teaching-racism.

93 *"The heart of our nation's problem with race":* Mark Charles, "2020 Cam-

paign Announcement Video," 6:28, www.youtube.com/watch?v=
_livxZNCQeU.

93   *"victimized . . . and abused":* Kelsey West, "Interpretations of Hagar:
Pathway to Healing in the Wake of Sexual Assault," Augustana Digital
Commons, February 15, 2017, https://digitalcommons.augustana.edu/
cgi/viewcontent.cgi?article=1003&context=relgstudent.

94   *"We and our kings, our princes and our ancestors":* Daniel 9:8.

94   *to change one's mind:* Bible Study Tools, s.v. "metanoia," www
.biblestudytools.com/lexicons/greek/nas/metanoia.html.

94   *"stood in their places":* Nehemiah 9:2.

94   *"a sustained state of national mourning for black lives":* Claudia Rankine,
"The Condition of Black Life Is One of Mourning," *The Fire This
Time,* ed. Jesmyn Ward (New York: Scribner, 2016), 155.

94   *In 2010, the government of Cameroon funded a visit to that nation:* Regina
Vaughn, "Bimbe: Will the Circle Be Closed?" *Exposing Bimbia: The
Transatlantic Slave Trade and the Cameroon Historic Diaspora,* Lisa Au-
brey, ed., http://exposingbimbia.blogspot.com/p/related-works.html.

95   *"integral part of public school education":* "The JUST Act Report: Germany," U.S. Department of State, www.state.gov/reports/just-act
-report-to-congress/germany.

95   *to compensate slaveholders for the loss of their "property":* Kris Manjapra,
"D.C.'s Enslavers Got Reparations. Freed People Got Nothing," *Polit-
ico,* June 17, 2022, www.politico.com/news/magazine/2022/06/17/
washington-emancipation-day-00038824.

95   *"only if accompanied by a public truth-telling project":* Ereshnee Naidu-
Silverman, "What South Africa Can Teach the U.S. About Reparations,"
The Washington Post, June 25, 2019, www.washingtonpost.com/outlook/
2019/06/25/what-south-africa-can-teach-us-about-reparations.

95   *"turn[ing] from the bitter task of repenting our own sins":* C. S. Lewis,
"The Dangers of National Repentance," *God in the Dock* (Grand Rapids, Mich.: Eerdmans, 2014), 206.

96   *"If people use the word 'we' in confessional prayer":* Marvin D. Hinten,
"Dangerous Repentance in Modern America: A Contemporary Parallel
to Lewis's 'Dangers of National Repentance,'" *The Lamp-Post of the
Southern California C.S. Lewis Society* 36, no. 1 (2017): 22–27, www.jstor
.org/stable/48616163.

101 *the Black church . . . has long been a home for the project:* Esau McCaulley, "When Two Narratives Clash: The Development of Black Ecclesial Interpretation and Evangelical Triumphalism," Center for Pastor Theologians Conference, 2021, video, 18:20–19:00, https://centerforpastortheologians.vhx.tv/packages/confronting-racial-injustice-cpt-conference-2021/videos/session-5-esau-mccaulley-fc1.

102 *"White people really want this to be what reconciliation means":* Austin Channing Brown, *I'm Still Here: Black Dignity in a World Made for Whiteness* (New York: Convergent, 2018), 110.

105 *a study revealing that Black babies are less likely to die:* Brad N. Greenwood et al., "Physician-Patient Racial Concordance and Disparities in Birthing Mortality for Newborns," *Proceedings of the National Academy of Sciences* 117, no. 35, August 17, 2020, https://doi.org/10.1073/pnas.1913405117.

109 *a group of well-intentioned White volunteers could not manage:* Jeremy Taylor, *The Wisdom of Your Dreams: Using Dreams to Tap into Your Unconscious and Transform Your Life* (New York: Penguin, 1992), 89–99.

110 *Robert Monson posted on Twitter:* Robert the Low Vibrational Contemplative (@robertjmonson), "This might seem small . . ." Twitter, May 17, 2021, 6:57 P.M., mobile.twitter.com/robertjmonson/status/1394457116765605889.

111 *"8:55 A.M.: . . . I am asked three times if I need help":* Brown, *I'm Still Here*, 71–77.

113 *"Shame can be a catalyst and a teacher":* myisha t hill, *Heal Your Way Forward: The Co-Conspirator's Guide to an Antiracist Future* (Chicago: Row House, 2022), 19.

115 *"This is for their joy":* Leigh Ann Erickson, "What Should We Teach Our White Students?," video, 25:15, www.youtube.com/watch?v=OwK3_KistZ8.

Chapter Seven: The Pastor

117 *"the alleged statute of this territory":* Theophilus Magruder v. Jacob Vanderpool Case Documents, B 122, Special Collections & University Archives, University of Oregon Libraries, Eugene, Oregon, https://scua.uoregon.edu/repositories/2/resources/1215.

119   *"in the second place, that the complaint":* Theophilus Magruder v. Jacob *Vanderpool* Case Documents.

120   *we all hail from Africa:* Ian Tattersall, "Human origins: Out of Africa," PNAS, September 22, 2009, www.pnas.org/doi/10.1073/pnas .0903207106.

121   *primarily concerned with power:* I'm sure there are many people who have made this observation, but the person who pointed it out to me, in conversation, was my mentor and professor Lauren Winner.

122   *"preached 13 sermons; delivered two lectures":* Ezra Fisher, *Correspondence of the Reverend Ezra Fisher: Pioneer Missionary of the American Baptist Home Mission Society in Indiana, Illinois, Iowa and Oregon* (London: Forgotten Books, 2018), 64.

123   *"Everything is to be done":* Fisher, *Correspondence,* 70.

123   *"If I have one object":* Fisher, *Correspondence,* 61.

123   *"some from China":* Fisher, *Correspondence,* 170.

123   *"Nothing would induce me":* Fisher, *Correspondence,* 278.

123   *"$1000 worth of gold":* Fisher, *Correspondence,* 282.

124   *"At this period in my life":* Fisher, *Correspondence,* 295.

124   *"All kinds of labor":* Fisher, *Correspondence,* 297.

124   *"We shall much need classical books":* Fisher, *Correspondence,* 297.

124   *"Our whole territory is materially suffering":* Fisher, *Correspondence,* 317.

125   *"Unless we are visited":* Fisher, *Correspondence,* 438.

128   *"In the matter of the Complaint":* Theophilus Magruder v. Jacob Vanderpool Case Documents.

130   *"Ezra Fisher was a strong anti-slavery man":* Ezra Fisher et al, *Correspondence of the Reverend Ezra Fisher; Pioneer Missionary of the American Baptist Home Mission Society in Indiana, Illinois, Iowa and Oregon* (Portland, Or: N.p., 1919), Linfield College Archives.

132   *"I am not, nor have ever been, in favor of bringing about":* "Mr. Lincoln and Negro Equality," *The New York Times,* December 28, 1860, www .nytimes.com/1860/12/28/archives/mr-lincoln-and-negro-equality .html.

Chapter Eight: From Silence to Self-Disclosure

133   *"The American church has yielded the prophetic voice":* Mark Charles and Soong-Chan Rah, *Unsettling Truths: The Ongoing, Dehumanizing Legacy of the Doctrine of Discovery* (Downers Grove, Ill.: InterVarsity, 2019), 9.

134   *"Who did it? Who threw that bomb?":* Charles Morgan, in Jemar Tisby, *The Color of Compromise: The Truth About the American Church's Complicity in Racism* (Grand Rapids, Mich.: Zondervan, 2019), 14.

134   *"We will have to repent in this generation":* Dr. Martin Luther King, Jr., "Letter from Birmingham Jail," August 1963, www.csuchico.edu/iege/_assets/documents/susi-letter-from-birmingham-jail.pdf.

138   *"Without being blessed with special mental or intellectual ability":* Lyman E. Latourette, *Latourette Annals in America* (self-pub., 1954), 119.

138   *"That they reached America with difficulty":* Latourette, *Latourette Annals,* 66.

139   *"a Negro wench to his wife":* Latourette, *Latourette Annals,* 56.

139   *"Sheldon's reference to genetics":* Latourette, *Latourette Annals,* 96–97.

141   *"that a negro, Chinaman or Indian has no right":* George Lawson, in K. Keith Richard, "Unwelcome Settlers: Black and Mulatto Oregon Pioneers," *Oregon Historical Quarterly* 84, no. 1 (Spring 1983): 29–55, www.jstor.org/stable/20613888.

143   *"He didn't say a single thing":* Osheta Moore, *Dear White Peacemakers* (Independence, Mo.: Herald, 2021), 76.

143   *"because of the church's silence":* Moore, *Dear White Peacemakers,* 78.

147   *a YouTube video made by Phil Vischer:* Phil Vischer, "Race in America," Holy Post, YouTube video, www.youtube.com/watch?v=AGUwcs9qJXY.

149   *"Forgiveness does not contradict the pursuit of justice":* Tim Keller, "What Too Little Forgiveness Does To Us," *The New York Times,* December 3, 2022, www.nytimes.com/2022/12/03/opinion/tim-keller-forgiveness.html.

Chapter Nine: The Exile

152   *"The law prohibiting negroes and mulattoes":* "The Black Law," *Weekly Oregon Statesman,* September 2, 1851, www.newspapers.com/clip/14800451/the-black-law.

152   *reprinted in newspapers as far away as Woodville, Mississippi:* "The Black

Law," *Woodville Republican*, November 25, 1851, 1, www.newspapers
.com/image/334857865/?terms=black%20law&match=1.

152 *"Even in the so-called free territory of Oregon"*: "Abner Hunt Francis,"
Oregon Secretary of State website, https://sos.oregon.gov/archives/
exhibits/black-history/Pages/families/francis.aspx.

153 *the largest Ku Klux Klan chapter west of the Mississippi*: Ben Bruce, "The
Rise and Fall of the Ku Klux Klan in Oregon During the 1920s," *Voces
Novae* 11 (2019), Chapman University, 1, https://digitalcommons
.chapman.edu/cgi/viewcontent.cgi?article=1126&context=
vocesnovae.

153 *"the Whitest city in America"*: Alana Semuels, "The Racist History of
Portland, the Whitest City in America," *The Atlantic*, July 22, 2016,
www.theatlantic.com/business/archive/2016/07/racist-history
-portland/492035.

154 *twelfth highest number of hate crimes*: "Number of Hate Crime Of-
fenses in the United States in 2020, by State," Statista, www.statista
.com/statistics/737930/number-of-hate-crimes-in-the-us-by
-motivation.

154 *the third-most per capita*: "Hate Crimes Surge Across Pacific Northwest
According to New FBI Data," ADL Pacific Northwest, August 30,
2021, https://seattle.adl.org/news/release-hate-crimes-surge-across
-pacific-northwest-according-to-new-fbi-data.

154 *more than 686,000 Oregonians voted*: Conrad Wilson, "Oregonians Remove Slavery Language from State Constitution, Though by 'Shock-
ingly Close' Margin," Oregon Public Broadcasting, November 10,
2022, www.opb.org/article/2022/11/10/oregon-election-removing
-slavery-language-from-state-constitution-passes.

159 *"gave birth to the first child born in the Oregon Country"*: I originally read
these descriptions of the importance of the names painted on the Capitol
walls on a state website that has since been taken down.

162 *"The Committee on Janitors"*: "A Clean Sweep of Janitors," *San Francisco
Examiner*, January 31, 1883, 1, https://sfexaminer.newspapers.com/
image/457607096.

167 *to "heal the land"*: Holly Bartholomew, "Grande Ronde Names Site at
Willamette Falls 'Tumwata Village'," *West Linn Tidings*, September 9,
2022, www.westlinntidings.com/news/grande-ronde-names-site-at

-willamette-falls-tumwata-village/article_17cddoab-2afe-524a-97b5
-c3829cdcb4b5.html.

Chapter Ten: From Exclusion to Community

168 *"'Sometimes I wonder,' said Thomas"*: Louise Erdrich, *The Night Watch-man* (New York: Harper Perennial, 2020), 141.

168 *"Rare is the ministry praying"*: Austin Channing Brown, *I'm Still Here: Black Dignity in a World Made for Whiteness* (New York: Convergent, 2018), 79.

168 *"Your name is not racist, it's Beloved"*: Osheta Moore, *Dear White Peace-makers* (Independence, Mo.: Herald, 2021), 63.

169 *"This community is in a period of transition"*: Denyse McGriff, in Ken Boddie, "Oregon City Makes History Electing Its First Mayor of Color," KOIN: Eye on NW Politics, August 28, 2022, interview, 00:44, www.koin.com/nwpolitics/oregon-city-makes-history-electing-its-first-mayor-of-color/#:~:text=(KOIN)%20%E2%80%94%20Denyse%20McGriff%20made,in%20Tillamook%20and%20other%20Communities.

169 *"White people are the most segregated"*: Heather McGhee, *The Sum of Us: What Racism Costs Everyone and How We Can Prosper Together* (New York: One World, 2021), 168.

169 *"entirely white"*: McGhee, *The Sum of Us*, 175.

172 *"I would not hesitate to say"*: Martin Luther King, Jr., "Letter from Bir-mingham Jail," August 1963, www.csuchico.edu/iege/_assets/documents/susi-letter-from-birmingham-jail.pdf.

173 *"White people . . . have suffered greatly"*: Wendell Berry, *The Hidden Wound* (Berkeley: Counterpoint, 1989), 1.

173 *"Racial segregation afflicts white children"*: Derrick Bell, *Silent Covenants: Brown v. Board of Education and the Unfulfilled Hopes for Racial Reform* (Oxford: Oxford University Press, 2004), 23.

173 *"There is a psychic and emotional cost"*: McGhee, *The Sum of Us*, xxii.

173 *"moral cost of racism"*: McGhee, *The Sum of Us*, 222.

174 *None of the White residents knew how to fish*: "The Clackamas People," www.usgennet.org/usa/or/county/clackamas/clackamas.html.

174 *"Why did these men not know me . . . ?"*: Willie James Jennings, *The*

Christian Imagination: Theology and the Origins of Race (New Haven: Yale University Press, 2010), 4.

175 *"the exercise of an imaginative capacity":* Jennings, *The Christian Imagination,* 6.

175 *"Understanding racism's harm upon White people":* Chanequa Walker-Barnes, *I Bring the Voices of My People* (Grand Rapids, Mich.: Eerdmans, 2019), 131.

181 *"a great cloud of witnesses":* Hebrews 12:1.

Epilogue: After Repentance

181 *"see through a glass, darkly":* 1 Corinthians 13:12, KJV.

183 *"But how much do you like white people?":* Kent Nerburn, *Neither Wolf nor Dog: On Forgotten Roads with an Indian Elder,* 25th Anniversary Edition (New York: New World Library, 2019), 16.

185 *Jesus's prayer for the unity of the church:* See John 17:22–23.

186 *"a great multitude":* Revelation 7:9.

186 *"I . . . liked the picture in Revelation where all the nations and tribes":* Athabascan chief, in Richard Twiss, *Rescuing the Gospel from the Cowboys: A Native American Expression of the Jesus Way* (Downers Grove, Ill.: InterVarsity, 2015), 117–18.

187 *"There is a river":* Psalm 46:4.

187 *Ezekiel the prophet saw this river in a vision:* See Ezekiel 47:1–12.

188 *In John's vision, the river of the water of life:* See Revelation 22:1–5.

188 *"Behold! . . . There will be no more death":* Revelation 21:4–5.

Index

slavery, 12–15, 24, 44, 46–48, 59–61,
 65, 90–91, 92, 95, 121, 130–33, 154
Slavin, Nancy, 161, 176, 192
Smith, Christian, 146, 195
Smith, Delazon, 158
Smith, Zadie, 31, 197
South Africa, 95
Spain, 9
Sprigg, Thomas, 64, 66
Showing Up for Racial Justice, 61,
 175, 176, 192
Stanley, John Mix, 165
Statesman. See Oregon Statesman
Stewart, Taylor, 176, 177, 179, 192
Stocks, Zachary, 36, 161, 179, 192
Sullivan, Shannon, 175
sundown state, 15
Supaman, 88
Susan, enslaved by the author's
 family, 56, 57, 59, 62, 63, 68
Sutherland, Ross, 164, 192
Swinton, John, 180

T

Taylor, Jeremy, 109
Taylor, Quintard, 14
Thompson, Gregory, 51, 196
Tisby, Jemar, xxiii, 30, 133, 134, 197
trial
 of Jacob Vanderpool, xxi, 17, 34,
  37, 42, 51, 71, 73, 74, 81, 82, 89,
  91, 116–17, 119–21, 125–26, 128,
  152, 158
 of William and Ezra Johnson, 74,
  77–79, 82

Trump White House, 92
Tucker, Alonzo, 141, 176
Twiss, Richard, 184, 186, 197

U

United Kingdom, 180
University of Oregon Special
 Collections Library, 51

V

Vanderpool, Amelia, 34, 163
Vanderpool, Eliza, 34, 163
Vanderpool, Jacob, 31–32, 55, 64, 87,
 132, 133
 business, 18, 35–36, 80, 151–52
 case brought by Theophilus
  Magruder, 37–40, 44, 47–50,
  74
 case file, 51, 53–54, 70–71
 custody, 73, 81–82, 85
 early life, 33–35
 exile, xii, xx, xxi, 80, 90, 124, 141,
  153, 154, 174
 late life, 161–64
 location, 164–67
 memorial, 176–79
 racial heritage, 17–18, 120–21
 trial. *See* trial
Vanderpool, Jane, 34, 163
Vanderpool, Martin, 34, 163,
 164
Vanderpool, Mary, 162–63
Virginia, 44, 46–48
Vischer, Phil, 147

About the Author

SARAH L. SANDERSON holds a master of fine arts in creative nonfiction from Seattle Pacific University, a master's in teaching from Seattle University, and a bachelor of English and philosophy from Wheaton College. For the past eight years, she and her family—including her husband, their four children, her brother, and the family's two dogs—have made their home in Oregon. These days, her pursuits include writing, speaking, teaching creative writing, learning to pray, and building the beloved community.

looking forward to the time when he would send for his young family to join him in Oregon—he had not yet met his baby boy. The day Jacob kissed his wife and toddler daughters goodbye, Eliza would have been approximately seven months pregnant.

What did Jacob Vanderpool dream of on his way to Oregon? What flooded his mind night after night as he lay swinging in his hammock while the ship creaked and rocked to the rhythm of the sea that had swallowed so many of his mother's people? What occupied his thoughts as he loaded cargo in the port cities of North America, or hoisted the rigging in the Caribbean Islands of his birth, or swabbed the decks off the coast of South America, or pumped out the bilge in the treacherous waters around Cape Horn, or kept watch as the crew tacked north and prepared to re-span two continents? In the New York City that Vanderpool had left behind, "whites saw blacks as a separate and unequal group." Did he imagine that in Oregon he might finally discover a land where his children could run free? As he lay among his fellow sailors, breathing in the salt- and sweat-laced dark, did he already plan to open a boarding house? It was a profession he would have known well, given the "strong links between mariners and victuallers." Did Vanderpool hope to settle himself on land, rather than at sea, so he would no longer have to leave those four precious lives behind?

All we know is that when Jacob Vanderpool arrived in Oregon City, he left his ship's employ. He established the Oregon Saloon and Boarding House on Main Street, opposite the *Statesman* office.* He furnished meals at the regular hours for seventy-five

---

*Some historians, such as Elizabeth McLagan, author of *Peculiar Paradise: A History of Blacks in Oregon, 1788–1940*, have placed Vanderpool in Oregon's present-day capital of

cents. Persons from the country were invited to call. All might have been well if one of the boarding houses down the street had not acquired new management.

Boarding houses were a regular feature of the nineteenth-century urban American landscape. Walt Whitman wrote in 1842 that such disparate characters as "lieutenants, loafers, ladies, lack-brains, and lawyers . . . all 'go out to board.'" With the steady stream of settlers all passing through on their way to claim their acres of farmland, Oregon City could surely have supported each of its several boarding houses. But when the new proprietor of the Main Street House surveyed his business competition, he apparently decided that one of his rivals would need to be eliminated.

He singled out Jacob Vanderpool.

Enter a new character into the drama of Jacob Vanderpool's life: Theophilus Magruder. The case that would forever stand on United States history books as the only time a person of African descent was prosecuted, convicted, and punished solely for the crime of being himself—not driving while Black, or running while Black, or shopping while Black, but simply *existing* while Black—

Salem rather than Oregon City. The confusion seems to arise from the fact that Vanderpool locates himself, in his ad, "across the street from the Statesman offices," and the *Statesman* has been headquartered in Salem since 1853. However, in 1851—the year Vanderpool operated his business, ran his advertisements, and endured the court case brought against him—the *Statesman* operated out of Oregon City. So Jacob Vanderpool must have been there too. Court documents also stated that Vanderpool "resides in Oregon City." Zachary Stocks, director of Oregon Black Pioneers, agreed by email, "All evidence points to Oregon City."

was not brought by any state (or, in this case, territory) authority. The case was brought by a single private citizen. *Theophilus Magruder v. Jacob Vanderpool.*

Despite the fact that the second version of Oregon's exclusion laws was already on the books, a handful of African Americans were living in Oregon at the time, scattered throughout the territory, and no one had pressed charges against any of them. Jacob Vanderpool might well have lived out his years in Oregon City as the proprietor of the Oregon Saloon and Boarding House, unbothered by anybody, were it not for the interference of Theophilus Magruder.

This is not to say that the law was toothless until Vanderpool just happened to unluckily run across one proverbial bad apple. Even before Vanderpool arrived in Oregon, the exclusion laws had already begun to accomplish their intended work; they had deterred at least one group of Black settlers from entering the Territory at all. George Washington Bush and his family heard about the law and turned north, forming the first permanent American settlement in the present-day Seattle area. Unfortunately, Vanderpool's case opened the door for other court cases. Just weeks after the Vanderpool trial, a pair of brothers in the Portland area, Abner and I.B. Francis, were also indicted for breaking the Exclusion Law. Later, when the boundaries of the Oregon Territory shifted to include present-day Washington State, George Washington Bush—the man who had attempted to steer clear of Oregon—was also tried for breaking the exclusion laws.

The difference for both Bush and the Francises was that, unlike Jacob Vanderpool, they had powerful White friends. Though justice should not depend on proximity to White friends, for Bush and the Francises, it made all the difference. Bush's friends wrote to Congress, which granted legal residence specifically and only to George Washington Bush in 1855. The Francises were saved from expulsion at the last minute by a petition signed by more than two hundred of their White neighbors. So, while Vanderpool remains the only person actually expelled from Oregon for breaking the exclusion laws, he was hardly the only person affected by them.

But why, specifically, *Theophilus Magruder v. Jacob Vanderpool*? One hundred seventy years on, we can only speculate as to Theophilus Magruder's reasons for pressing charges against Jacob Vanderpool. But a ready motive presents itself when we learn that on July 8, 1851, just a month after Vanderpool first ran his own ad, Theophilus Magruder took out a notice in the *Oregon Statesman:*

> We, the undersigned, having leased the "Main Street
> House" of this city, beg leave to inform the citizens and the
> public in general, that we hope, by a strict attention to our
> Table, Bed-rooms, and whatever may conduce to the com-
> fort of our friends, to merit a share of their patronage. The
> Main Street House is being thoroughly repaired, and will be
> opened for the public to-day, when we will be happy to see
> as many of our friends as may do us the favor to call.

This was not Magruder's first attempt at hotel-keeping. In 1847, Magruder had operated the City Hotel. One traveler who spent the night there in 1848 wrote in his diary that Magruder's first hotel was full of guests who were "dusty and roughly dressed . . . jovial,